Felix Brunner, Thomas Rudolph
Toward Cross-Channel Management

I0041262

Felix Brunner, Thomas Rudolph

Toward Cross-Channel Management

A Comprehensive Guide for Retail Firms

DE GRUYTER
OLDENBOURG

ISBN 978-3-11-055389-5
e-ISBN (PDF) 978-3-11-041716-6
e-ISBN (EPUB) 978-3-11-041722-7

Library of Congress Cataloging-in-Publication Data
A CIP catalog record for this book has been applied for at the Library of Congress.

Bibliographic information published by the Deutsche Nationalbibliothek
The Deutsche Nationalbibliothek lists this publication in the Deutsche Nationalbibliografie;
detailed bibliographic data are available on the Internet at http://dnb.dnb.de.

© 2017 Walter de Gruyter GmbH, Berlin/Munich/Boston
This volume is text- and page-identical with the hardback published in 2015.
Cover illustration: LDProd/iStock/Thinkstock
Printing and binding: CPI books GmbH, Leck

♾ Printed on acid-free paper
Printed in Germany

www.degruyter.com

Contents

List of Figures

List of Tables

To our families & friends

Preface

"It is not the ship so much as the skillful sailing that
assures the prosperous voyage."
George William Curtis

This book deals with the greatest challenge in retailing at present – the fundamental change in shopping behavior when consumers interchangeably use various online and offline channels – a phenomenon that is referred to as cross-channel shopping. Because digital devices such as smartphones and tablets enable consumers to ubiquitously access the Internet, and inspire them to switch between online and offline channels, cross-channel shopping is the reality that firms must face in many retail industries. Even though this change in consumer behavior offers great potential, specifically for multi-channel players to successfully fight back against online pure players, it also imposes significant risk. With the greater alignment of channels, the complexity of the overall business model increases, and may negatively affect the cost position of the firm. This book presents specific management tools and templates in order to analyze how multi-channel incumbents can manage the firm-wide transformation process to successfully cater to the demands of cross-channel shoppers – an approach we call cross-channel management.

The book is based on results from studies conducted over the past five years, for which we carried out intensive research on the topic of cross-channel management. These studies include, *first*, insights from the PhD project of Dr. Felix Brunner, involving 71 top and middle managers of nine multi-channel firms from different retail industries. *Second*, we use results from cross-channel shopping studies carried out in 2014 and 2011, as well as Internet usage studies from 2013 and 2011, all published by Professor Thomas Rudolph. All four studies were conducted by the Institute of Retail Management, and with a study population developed from a representative sample of consumers from Switzerland, Germany, and Austria. *Third*, we include ideas and conclusions raised during a cross-channel management seminar – a six-module course for top executives from the Executive School of the University of St.Gallen that involved twelve top managers from various retail firms.

This book targets top managers, who are looking for new insights on how to transform their firms in a move toward cross-channel management, and middle managers who are directly confronted with changes in consumer behavior, such as heads of e-commerce and marketing divisions, who seek advice on how to successfully integrate their online and offline channels. As well, the audience for this book includes a generalized group of managers who are interested in the topic as a way to better understand the business complexity behind the phenomenon of cross-channel retailing. The final group for whom our book is useful consists of both executive and non-executive students, from all levels, who want to learn how to tackle this disruptive change in consumer behavior from strategic and managerial points of view.

Our successful completion of this project owes a debt to a network of inspiring and brilliant people who have offered valuable support during the last five years of research. In addition to offering sincere appreciation to all who participated in our studies – particularly the top and middle managers from various retail firms – we thank Ms. Kristina Kleinlercher from the Institute of Retail Management (IRM-HSG) for her great support reviewing and editing our manuscript, Dr. Deborah Nester from Northwest Florida State College for the proofreading, and Mrs. Anja Ludwig from De Gruyter for the final editing.

St. Gallen, October 2014   Thomas Rudolph and Felix Brunner

Summary

New digital devices such as smartphones and tablets enable consumers to ubiquitously access the Internet and inspire them to switch between online and offline channels when shopping – a phenomenon that research on consumer behavior terms cross-channel shopping. For multi-channel incumbents, this change in consumer behavior offers great potential as it may entail a long-awaited answer to the increasing pressure from fast-growing pure online players. While retailers ran their online and offline channels as separated profit-centers in the era of multi-channel management, today, retail incumbents aspire to integrate their channels to offer compelling switching opportunities among all online and offline channels – an approach we coin cross-channel management. Addressing cross-channel shoppers may come at a high price for multi-channel firms: With greater alignment of channels comes an overall rise in business model complexity which can only be tackled by installing a firm-wide strategic change process. However, multi-channel incumbents often hesitate to integrate their online and offline channels to cater to the new consumer behavior as they struggle to manage this firm-wide change process. Set against this transformative background, this book offers insight into how firms can overcome said inertia and successfully transform their current channel specific business model to a much more integrated system of online and offline channels. In doing so, the present contribution scrutinizes one of today's major challenges in retailing and provides answers to the following questions:

1. Why should firms in retailing try to develop a better understanding of cross-channel management and to what extent does this step into the digital world affect your company?
2. How should firms approach cross-channel management from a strategic perspective and what kind of decisions have to be taken in order to achieve a competitive advantage through this new concept?
3. Which tools and frameworks might help to implement cross-channel management properly?

This book examines the resourceful integration of online and offline channels in retailing in practice. All our recommendations are based on several research projects that have been conducted during the last four years. In addition, insights from numerous discussions with experienced retail practitioners found their way into this book. We strongly believe that cross-channel management is one of the most fundamental challenges affecting retail companies across the globe. Yet, due to the digital revolution, cross-channel management is not only a major concern for retailers. More and more manufactures are harnessing the Internet by launching their own digital distribution channels, becoming retailers themselves. Even as we begin this discussion, we have to concede that cross-channel management is no easy task. Most of the companies scrutinized in our research struggled considerably with the transformation process, having to overcome various unforeseen challenges along the way. There are many obstacles to overcome along this challenging transformation process – a process during which even excellent project management cannot avoid mistakes. However, there are two major reasons why companies should take the leap and look for their most effective path toward cross-channel management. First, most companies see opportunities for growth with existing customers. They aim to offer a seamless and enhanced shopping experience that fosters customer relations. Second, ignoring cross-channel management poses a significant threat of loosing market share. Industries where cross-channel management is already well developed – best exemplified by sports, entertainment, apparel, and consumer electronics – reveal that frontrunners in cross-channel management may have struggled, but many have been successful in capturing market share before their competirors could make the change.

This book offers guidelines for developing the path toward cross-channel management, with the goal of growing with existing customers as well as attracting new ones. The *first chapter* offers a brief and comprehensive overview on the cross-channel shopping phenomenon and explains the major problems and challenges retailers face when starting to integrate their online with their offline channels. The *second chapter* introduces a typology of strategic channel modes and derives three different strategic development paths for multi-channel incumbents to transform their business model toward a cross-channel setup. The *third chapter* introduces the *Cross-Channel Evaluator* and the *Cross-Channel Flywheel* as two hands-on management tools to successfully manage the transformation process toward cross-channel management.

1 Introduction

"Don't fight forces, use them."
R. Buckminster Fuller

With the recent development of new technological devices such as smartphones and tablets, and with the rise of Web 2.0 technologies, for retailers the Internet has become much more than a facilitating tool for information gathering and communication (PWC, 2013). In fact, an increasing number of consumers take advantage of these new technological devices, shopping at any time they wish and effortlessly switching between online and offline channels. Thus, consumers use online channels (e.g., online shops or in-store terminals) as well as traditional channels (e.g., bricks-and-mortar stores or catalogues) interchangeably, and along all phases of the buying process (search, purchasing, and post-purchasing phases). Research on multi-channel marketing refers to such consumer behavior as *cross-channel shopping* (e.g., Verhoef, Neslin and Vroomen, 2007; Chatterjee, 2010). Results from two empirical studies emphasize this change in consumer behavior by showing that, currently, 20 percent of German and Swiss shoppers are already cross-channel shoppers, preferring to switch between online and offline shopping channels (Rudolph et al., 2013).

1.1 The Rise of Cross-Channel Shopping

The following story of "Mike" demonstrates how new technological devices are revolutionizing customers' shopping behavior. Mike, 28, works as a project manager in the pharmaceutical industry. In addition to his laptop, he also possesses one personal smartphone, one business smartphone, and a tablet PC. On Thursday night after a long business day, he is watching television and notices a commercial for a well-known outdoor sporting goods brand. This advertisement reminds him that he is in dire need of new hiking boots for a two-day hiking trip with his girlfriend. Still on his couch, he takes his tablet PC, browses through the advertised websites to find which retailer in his area has the specific brand available. He sees that the outdoor sporting goods retailer *Outdoor Guy*[1] has the brand in stock and offers a function on its webpage that allows him to arrange for a personal shopping appointment. Thus, with only two clicks, he makes a reservation for in-store assistance the following day at 11 a.m., when he has free time between two business meetings. Through the website, he selects five different pairs of boots he wants to try on during his store visit. When he enters the local branch of the sporting goods store, the sales representative already waits with the reserved boots, and also shows him two additional models in

---

[1] Fictitious name.

the collection that had just arrived. After a few minutes, Mike considers a nice pair of boots that seems to match his needs. However, it is a brand that he has never heard of and he is not sure whether to entirely trust the salesperson. He grabs his smartphone and uses the retailer's barcode scan function to find a wealth of online information, videos, and customer reviews. Even though the online information corresponds with the information provided by the store sales representative, he still thinks he might get a better deal if he buys the boots online, so does not make a purchase. That evening he browses through a price comparison site and the retailer's website, where he is offered assistance from a customer service representative. He selects the "Call me now" button and receives a VoIP-call from the retailer's call-center agent. After an informative call, Mike is finally convinced that he has found the perfect boots and orders them online from the outdoor retailers' online shop. He is particularly pleased to note that the retailer offers free delivery, guaranteed within the next forty-eight hours, just in time for his hiking event.

Unfortunately, Mike's hiking trip turns out to be a nightmare – an hour into the steep climb he gets blisters because the shoes are too tight at the heel. On Sunday evening after the hiking trip, he calls the online-store support team to ask for advice. The call-center agent proposes another personal shopping visit to a store location that has what the retailer calls a foot-scan service. The call-center agent arranges a store appointment in the city where Mike is traveling for a business trip on Monday morning. Because he does not want to carry the unsatisfactory boots with him on his business trip, he decides to take advantage of the free shipping service and sends the boots back by mail – getting the full refund on his loyalty card account. On Monday, Mike is pleased when, as soon as he walks into the store, the sales representative knows who he is and that he needs assistance to select boots with a better fit. Using the newly installed three-dimensional foot-scan application on the sales clerk's tablet PC, Mike can choose between three different pairs of boots tailored to his needs. He selects a pair and, as compensation for the inconvenience caused by the ill-fitting shoe, receives an email with a ten-percent discount coupon on all apparel items, redeemable immediately through any of the retailer's sales channels. Because Mike cannot carry the boots with him to his next business meeting, he chooses to have them shipped home free of charge, along with a fleece jacket that he bought with his coupon.

A New Customer Group

In the preceding vignette, Mike's shopping behavior is not unusual, as it illustrates the current move toward cross-channel shopping behavior. The advent of the new shopping phenomenon has major implications for all retailers – multi-channel players, classic bricks-and-mortar players, and pure online players. On the one hand, based on evidence of channel-switching behavior, consumers seem to be less loyal to specific retailers, switching channels and retailers during the shopping process (Chiu et al., 2011). On the other hand, channel-switching consumers such as Mike are a particularly valuable and lucrative customer group. They spend more, on average, increasing their value over single-channel customers (Kushwaha and Shankar, 2008a; Neslin et al., 2006). Multi-channel retailers targeting this new customer group can achieve increased revenues if they are able to keep cross-channel customers loyal by offering channel-switching opportunities during the shopping process.

Our latest consumer survey based on close to 2,800 interviews in Austria, Germany and Switzerland proofs an increasing interest in the so-called cross-channel shopping. The following research findings urge managers from different industries to get a better understanding of consumer behavior in the digital world (Rudolph et al., 2014):

1. More than half of consumers know companies that sell products online and offline. The awareness of cross-channel retailers is rising.
2. More and more shoppers use different distribution channels when shopping for consumer electronics, furniture, textiles, cosmetics, shoes or even grocery. In 2014 26.5 percent visited the retailer's online-shop and the bricks-and-mortar store in their path to purchase.
3. On average among all categories 28.9 percent of consumers visited the retailer's online shop before purchasing the product in the retailer's bricks-and-mortar store. Research online and purchase offline, the so called ROPO-Effect, is becoming more popular.
4. In terms of touch points usage when shopping online shops are getting more important. 63.3 percent of cross-channel shoppers visit the retailer's online-shop in the purchasing process; 62.6 percent visit the retailers' bricks-and-mortar store (N = 2,780). Allthough the online-shop is visited more frequently in the purchasing process, the retailer's bricks-and-mortar store is still evaluated slightly more important for the purchasing decision.

Off course, our findings differ between retailing categories a lot. In consumer electronics, for example, the consumer decision journey compared to grocery purchases is much longer, consists of much more touch points and is more price driven. Therefore, each company should spend more attention to understand the consumer decision journey of their target groups. This journey was different 5 years ago and will be extended through cross-channel possibilities and more intense smartphone usage.

In order to compete with pure online players that contest their market shares, multi-channel retailers are highly challenged to harmonize their online and offline channels. If they manage to offer smooth shopping experiences and seamless switching opportunities across all online and offline channels of an integrated channel system, retailers will not only retain customer loyalty, but will also attract new cross-channel shoppers from other players (Zhang et al., 2010). However, despite the considerable potential inherent in the cross-channel shopper phenomenon, many multi-channel retailers struggle to successfully cater to this change in customer behavior.

Although almost all bricks-and-mortar retailers think that cross-channel management is a key for future success, only 46 percent have already defined a cross-channel strategy (BearingPoint, 2012). Even though the change in consumer behavior toward cross-channel shopping can be viewed as the most disruptive change in the retail environment since the advent of the discount phenomenon in the late 1960's, many multichannel incumbents have embarked on the pursuit of cross-channel management to actively defend their market shares against pure online players (PWC, 2013).

1.2 The Era of Cross-Channel Management

Research in channel retailing has evolved significantly in the last two decades moving from multiple channel management, to multi-channel management, to cross-channel management. Until 2000, *multiple channel management* simply referred to managing more than one distribution channel pipeline (Frazier, 1999). From the beginning of the digital age, around 1990, until 2010, *multi-channel management* indicated "a set of activities involved in selling merchandise or services to consumers through more than one channel" (Levy & Weitz, 2009). Since 2010, pure online retailers have steeply increased their market share (e.g., Amazon) and classic retailers have started to intertwine their online and offline channels (e.g., Apple) based on new technological devices that enable and inspire shoppers to switch between online and offline channels. A new era of channel management called *cross-channel management* was born. Compared to multi-channel management, cross-channel management goes one step further and can be described as management that deliberately focuses on the integra-

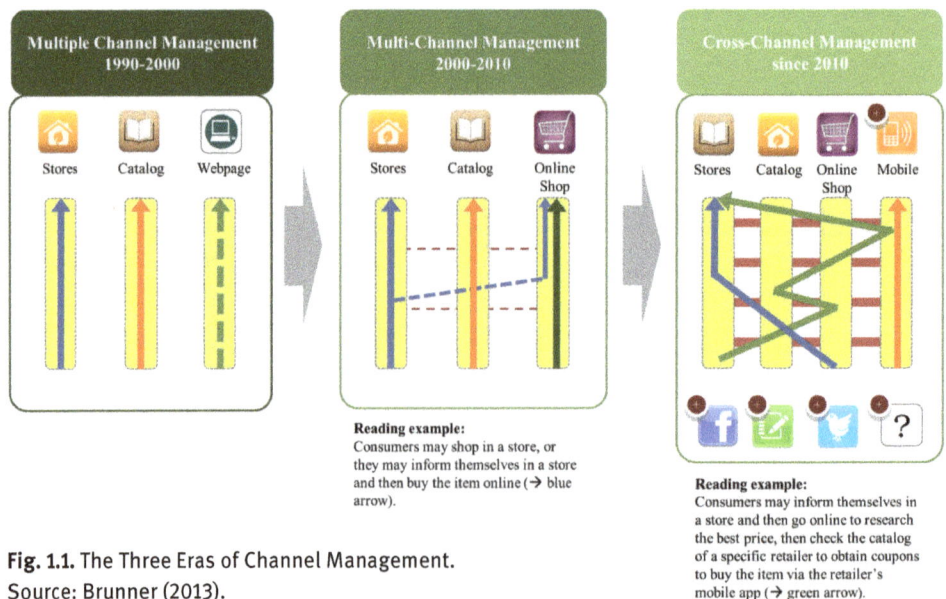

Reading example:
Consumers may shop in a store, or they may inform themselves in a store and then buy the item online (→ blue arrow).

Reading example:
Consumers may inform themselves in a store and then go online to research the best price, then check the catalog of a specific retailer to obtain coupons to buy the item via the retailer's mobile app (→ green arrow).

Fig. 1.1. The Three Eras of Channel Management.
Source: Brunner (2013).

tion of all online and offline channels in order to offer customers seamless switching opportunities across all channels (Zhang et al., 2010). Figure 1.1 illustrates the three eras of channel retailing.

On their journey toward channel integration, multi-channel retailers need to decide how to orchestrate their various consumer touch points. Thus, they must deal with the question of how to intertwine their online and offline distribution channels (e.g., stores, call center, webshop, mobile-device shop, or even Facebook) to be able to offer compelling switching opportunities to consumers (Zhang et al., 2010). However, they also need to think about how they can interlink classic, online, and social media

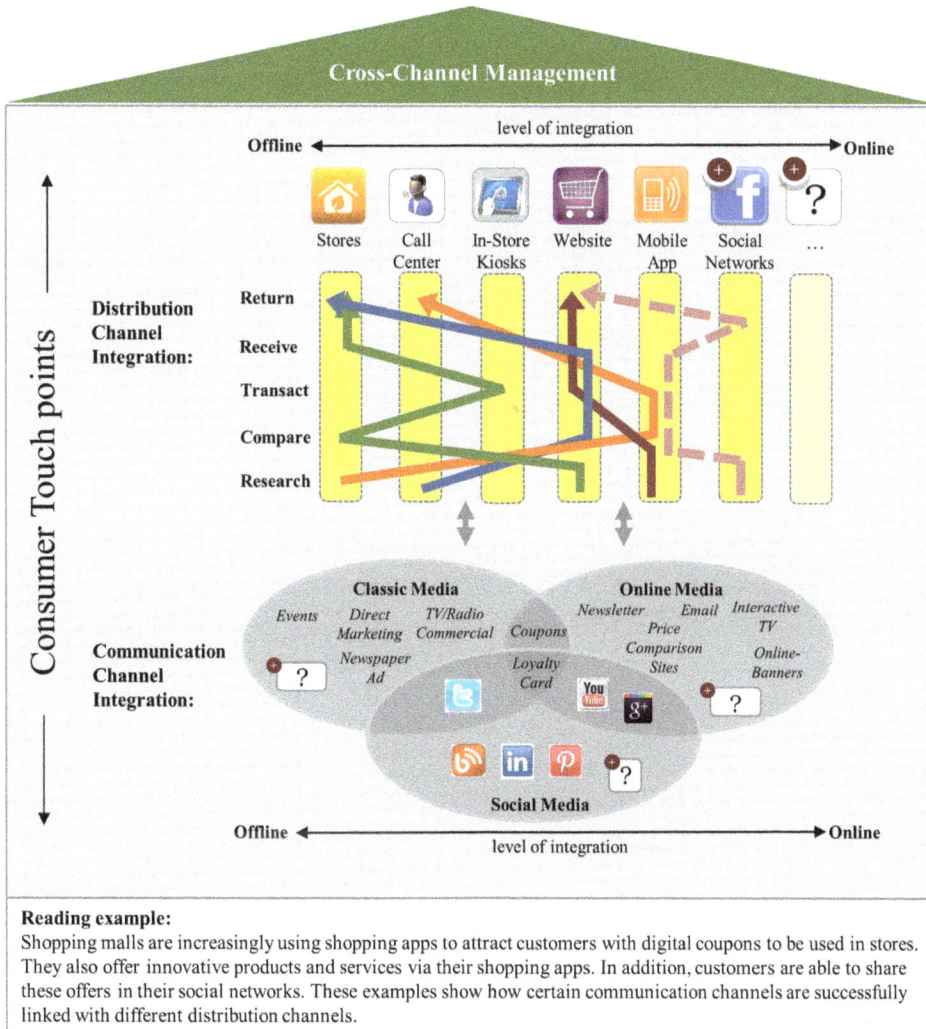

Reading example:
Shopping malls are increasingly using shopping apps to attract customers with digital coupons to be used in stores. They also offer innovative products and services via their shopping apps. In addition, customers are able to share these offers in their social networks. These examples show how certain communication channels are successfully linked with different distribution channels.

Fig. 1.2. The Two Distinctive Dimensions of Channel Integration.
Source: Brunner (2013).

communication channels (i.e., *classic:* events, flyers, television commercials; *online:* newsletters, coupons; *social:* tags, blogs, recommendations) to address and promote consumers' channel-switching behavior – for example, when customers use one distribution channel for research and another for purchasing (Frambach et al., 2007). To integrate their online and offline channels, therefore, multi-channel firms need to consider the two distinctive dimensions of distribution and communication. Figure 1.2 explains how these two dimensions allow for an intertwining of all consumer touch points.

1.3 The Managerial Perspective of Cross-Channel Management

Academics and practitioners alike show that channel integration is the key challenge for multi-channel retailers who seek to cater to the change in shopping behavior toward cross-channel shopping, and in the process must defend their market shares against pure online players (Neslin & Shankar, 2009; Zhang et al., 2010; PWC 2012; Roland Berger Strategy Consultants, 2013).

Extant research on multi-channel management has investigated the changes in consumer behavior by scrutinizing *cross-channel shoppers' satisfaction, loyalty, and channel migration* (e.g., Ansari et al., 2008), *cross-channel spending and segmentation* (e.g., Konus et al., 2008), *channel choice decisions* (e.g., Kushwaha & Shankar, 2008), *channel cannibalization* (e.g., Deleersnyder et al., 2002) and *marketing-mix decisions across channels* (e.g., Kushwaha & Shankar, 2008). However, other than this abundance of research on the cross-channel shopping phenomenon, very few studies have addressed the managerial challenges faced by multi-channel incumbents when striving for integration of their online and offline channels (e.g., Berger et al., 2006). In their review papers on the extensive research available on multi-channel management, Zhang et al. (2010), Neslin and Shankar (2009), and Rangaswamy and Van Bruggen (2005) identify the key areas for future research on cross-channel management from a managerial perspective. These are 1) dynamism of multi-channel strategies, 2) adaptation of organizational structure, 3) data integration, 4) consumer analytics, 5) performance metrics, and 6) cross-channel leadership.

In practice, many consulting firms have examined the characteristics of the new cross-channel shopper segment (e.g., PWC, 2013; Roland Berger Strategy Consultants, 2013). Consequently, practitioners are clearly ahead in dealing with the managerial challenges that the firm-wide transformation process toward channel integration poses. Previous studies have focused on the *multi-channel strategy process* (e.g., Accenture, 2010), *supply chain requirements* (e.g., Micros, 2011), and *cross-channel team structures* (e.g., Shop.org & J.C. Williams, 2008). Nonetheless, extant publications leave potential for future research on strategies to successfully transform the firm from a multi-channel approach to a cross-channel approach, the supply chain efficiencies

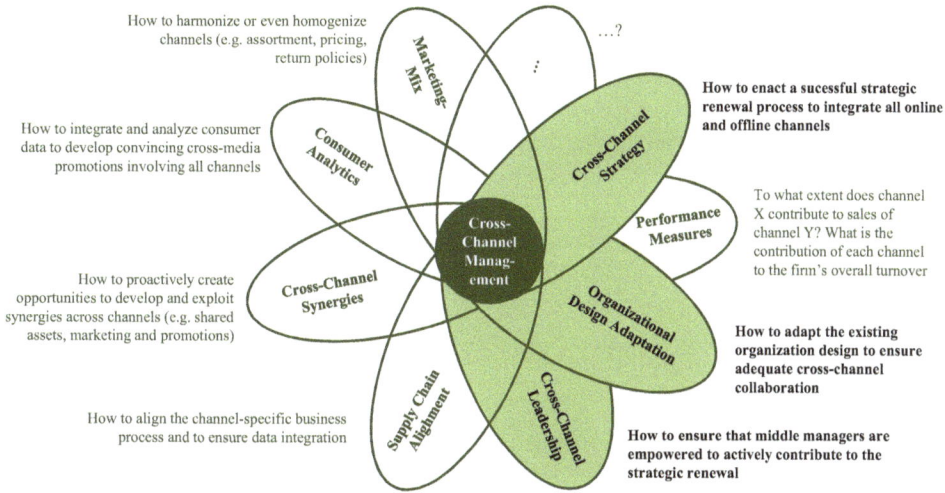

Fig. 1.3. Key Questions of Managerial Importance in the Field of Cross-Channel Management.
Source: Brunner (2013).

that are part of channel integration, and needed adaptations of the organizational design to ensure an appropriate level of cross-channel collaboration.

Figure 1.3 summarizes the key questions of managerial importance in the field of cross-channel management, and highlights the three topics that this book is mainly addressing. These are 1) the strategic perspective, 2) the structural perspective, and 3) the cultural perspective.

1.4 Objectives of This Book

Since the strategic renewal process toward cross-channel management can be qualified as a nascent field of research still in its formative stage, we were convinced that a holistic approach best fits our intent to examine and explain the impact of the cross-channel shopping phenomenon on today's multi-channel incumbents. For this, we apply a multiple case design (Eisenhardt, 1989; Yin, 2009) to address the following three objectives illustrated in Figure 1.4.

The basic motivation for multi-channel incumbents to adapt their somehwat separated channel configuration to a much more intertwined cross-channel approach is to address so-called loyal cross-channel shoppers, thereby retaining existing customers while gaining new customers from pure online players or other multi-channel retailers. Unlike competitive cross-channel shoppers who use a channel of firm X for information but buy the product in a channel of firm Y, or one-stop shoppers who obtain information and purchase the product in one channel only of firm X, loyal cross-channel shoppers remain with the same company, using various channels throughout the en-

1	To explain the change in consumer behavior and to visualize the relevance and key characteristics of the cross-channel shopping phenomenon → **Consumer Perspective: Chapter 1**
2	To examine and explain different strategic development paths for multichannel incumbents to successfully cater to the demands of cross-channel shoppers → **Strategie Perspective: Chapter 2**
3	To describe a set of managerial que stions to be answered sequentially, and to provide guidelines and frameworks in order to achieve a comprehensive and effective cross-channel management approach. → **Planning Perspective: Chapter 3**

Fig. 1.4. Objectives of this Book.
Source: Brunner (2013).

tire purchasing process (Neslin & Shankar, 2009). To successfully manage this firm-wide strategic change process toward cross-channel management, this book offers a set of guidelines following a holistic management-oriented approach to answer the following research question: *How do multi-channel retailers adapt their channel configuration in order to cater to the demands of cross-channel shoppers?* To address this research question, our book is structured as follows: In chapter 1, we focus on the customer perspective explaining the change of consumer behavior toward cross-channel shopping. In chapter 2, we focus on the strategic as well as the structural perspective and explain how different strategic development paths can be pursued to successfully establish cross-channel management. In chapter 3, we focus on the planning perspective and introduce different management tools and templates to organize and manage the firm-wide transformation process toward cross-channel management. Figure 1.5 embeds the three perspectives and visually conveys our goal of examining the micro-foundations of the firm-wide, top-driven strategic renewal process that multi-channel retailers face when striving for channel integration.

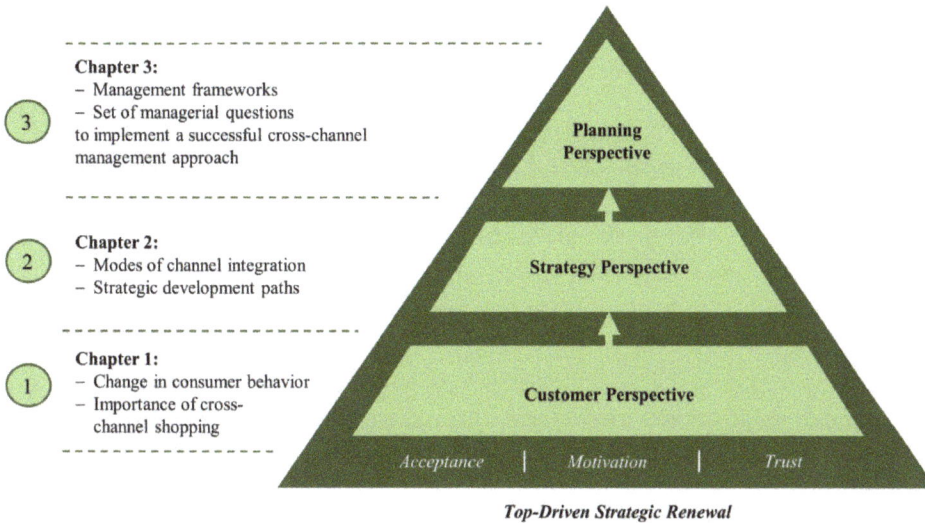

Chapter 3:
– Management frameworks
– Set of managerial questions
to implement a successful cross-channel
management approach

Chapter 2:
– Modes of channel integration
– Strategic development paths

Chapter 1:
– Change in consumer behavior
– Importance of cross-
channel shopping

Planning Perspective

Strategy Perspective

Customer Perspective

Acceptance | *Motivation* | *Trust*

Top-Driven Strategic Renewal

Fig. 1.5. Frame of Reference.
Source: Brunner (2013).

1.5 Recommendations Based on a Qualitative Research Design

A process perspective in research is crucial to understanding how multi-channel retailers can cater to the demands of the new cross-channel shoppers. We therefore use a qualitative research approach and employ a rigorous case study design. The sample consists of multi-channel retailers (their management teams of top, higher-middle, and lower-middle managers) that strive for channel integration. As is common in case study design, we combine elements of inductive theory (Glaser & Strauss, 1967) and structured methods (Eisenhardt, 1989). Therefore, we did not posit any a priori propositions in the early phases of the research process, but instead guided our research along three blocks of research questions derived from a thorough review of extant literature (Cavaye, 1996).

1.6 Case Study Design

Our case design embeds three units of analysis: (1) strategic renewal process, (2) changes in organizational design, and (3) top and middle management interaction. The first unit of analysis identifies *four channel integration modes* and derives *three strategic development paths* to cross-channel management. The second unit of analysis identifies *four routes of organizational design adaptation* to successfully cater to the demands of cross-channel shoppers. The third unit of analysis scrutinizes *top man-*

*agement leadership practices that empower middle manage*rs to contribute to strategic renewal initiatives.

1.7 Data Collection and Data Analysis

All ideas presented here originate from an extended research initiative on cross-channel management. From 2009 to 2013, we studied more than 25 retailers and worked with over 100 top and middle managers.

In an earlier study in 2010, conducted on the cross-channel shopping phenomenon, we surveyed more than 1,500 consumers in Switzerland and Germany to better understand consumer behavior movement toward cross-channel shopping. A further study in 2011 examined how retailers develop their online business alongside their store business, and how they managed first initiatives to interlink these two channel entities. In this study, we relied on a multiple case design, working with explorative interview data as well as secondary data collected from eight multi-channel players from six different countries (Austria, France, Germany, Switzerland, the U.K., and the U.S.[2]). Based on the case research, we learned that when multi-channel retailers need to set up a strategic change plan to intertwine online and offline channels, it is crucial that they distinguish between distribution- and communication-channel integration.

In our most recent study[3], we focused on specific multi-channel retailers in Switzerland and Germany that are considered to be pioneers in integrating their online and offline channels. We selected and thoroughly investigated the planning of the strategic change process of multi-channel retailers from different retail industries. In addition, we took into consideration the market settings of each retail industry, as well as the specific situation of the selected player within its industry. Our data collection procedure in this most recent study included a wide range of informants from top and middle management levels, which reduced information bias within individual respondent perspectives. We applied a triangulated approach (Yin, 2009) and, to allow for maximum richness and closeness to the research objective, we were thereby dependent on semi-structural interviews, short questionnaires, observations of top and middle management interactions, follow-up phone conversations, emails and secondary data sources such as strategy and change documents, organizational documentation, organization charts, press releases, customer survey results, website information, annual reports, and news articles (Martin & Eisenhardt, 2010). We conducted 78 semi-structured interviews with 71 top and middle managers from nine

---

2 Countries listed in alphabetical order.
3 Dissertation project: Brunner (2013): Towards Cross-Channel Management – Strategic, Structural, and Managerial Challenges for Multi-Channel Incumbents.

multi-channel firms. As recommended by Martin and Eisenhardt, interviews were transcribed within twenty-four hours after they were conducted (2010). As is typical in inductive case-based research (Eisenhardt, 1989; Eisenhardt & Graebner, 2007), we first built individual case write-ups that triangulated all collected data for each study (Jick, 1979). Second, relying on the seminal methodological studies by Eisenhardt (1989), Eisenhardt and Graebner (2007), and Miles and Huberman (1994), we conducted an iterative cross-case comparison for each article, following the replication logic of Yin (2009), and we performed paired case comparisons in order to build explanations and to draw cross-case conclusions (Eisenhardt, 1989). Third, after having developed conceptual constructs from preliminary cross-case results, we tested these constructs by analyzing the case data, emergent theory, and previous literature to validate and further refine the preliminary findings aimed at elaborating existing theoretical constructs (e.g., Martin & Eisenhardt, 2010). This most recent study – consisting of nine in-depth case studies – is the fundamental basis for most managerial recommendations of this book.

1.8 Nine Company Cases from Different Retail Industries

The selected multi-channel retailers were selected from the population of Swiss and German retailers who are striving to cater to the demands of cross-channel shoppers in the sectors Books and Entertainment, Apparel, Consumer Electronics, Sports and Outdoor, Furnitures, Fragrances, and Hunting and Apparel. These retail sub-industries were favored because previous studies qualified them as frontrunner retail industry segments for the firm-wide strategic renewal process of moving from multi-channel to cross-channel management (Emrich & Rudolph, 2010; PWC, 2012). After the study population was defined, we thoughtfully selected nine multi-channel retailers who initiated a firm-wide transformation process to intertwine their previously rather separated online and offline channels as a much more interlinked channel integration approach. However, the firms were situated in different phases of this top-driven firm-wide strategic renewal process. Our overall goal was to achieve a diverse sample that provided different possibilities for comparison, and that allowed for rich theoretical and generalizable conclusions across retail sub-industries. The sampling of firms and managers followed theoretical rather than statistical considerations (Glaser & Strauss, 1967; Pettigrew, 1990). Given our challenging overall research objective, this design required that case firms not only grant full access to all management levels, but also that they would give full disclosure of secondary data and would allow us to observe specific top and middle management interaction mechanisms. These restrictions further limited our choice, and resulted in the acquisition of nine Swiss and German multi-channel retailers as case firms. For reasons of confidentiality we have changed the names of those companies, and they are identified as Annapurna, Everest, K2, Kilimanjaro, Lhotse, Matterhorn, McKinley, Mont Blanc, and Zugspitze (see Figure 1.6).

High Level of Channel Integration:	Medium Level of Channel Integration:	Low Level of Channel Integration:

1 Matterhorn
TM interviews: 4
Higher MM interviews: 5
MM interviews: 2

4 K2
TM interviews: 2
Higher MM interviews: 4
MM interviews: 1

7 Annapurna
TM interviews: 3
Higher MM interviews: 5
MM interviews: 6

2 Mont Blanc
TM interviews: 2
Higher MM interviews: 6
MM interviews: 6

5 KcKinley
TM interviews: 2
Higher MM interviews: 1
MM interviews: 1

8 Everest
TM interviews: 3
Higher MM interviews: 4
MM interviews: 3

3 Lhotse
TM interviews: 2
Higher MM interviews: 2
MM interviews: 1

6 Zugspitze
TM interviews: 2
Higher MM interviews: 1
MM interviews: 1

9 Kilimanjaro
TM interviews: 1
Higher MM interviews: 2
MM interviews: 2

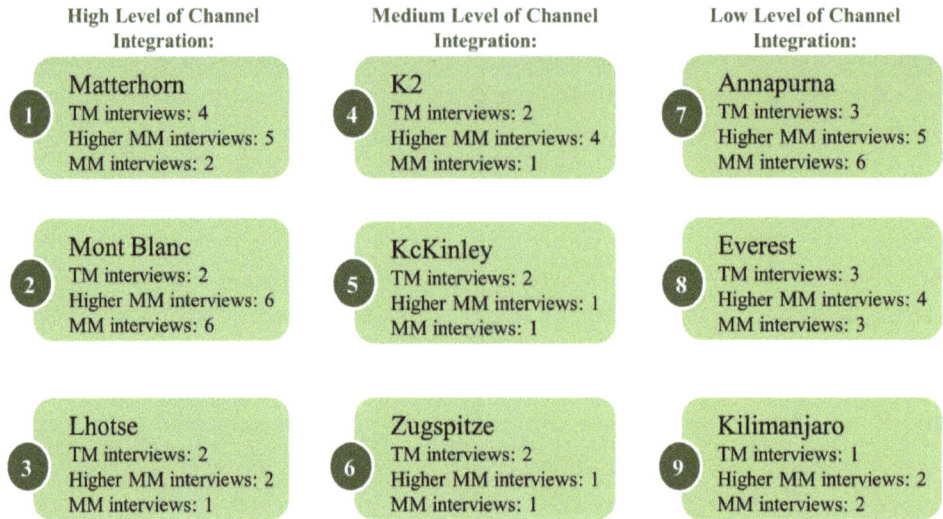

Fig. 1.6. Overview of Case Firms.
Source: Brunner (2013).

After establishing a research partnership with these firms we were granted access to firsthand information through interviews with top and middle managers.

Although our selected case firms tended to be more successful in their efforts toward channel integration compared to other multi-channel incumbents, they nevertheless showed a significant level of variation for all three research perspectives, thus ensuring the needed variance for inductive case-based theory elaboration.

In sum, 2,555 pages of interview transcripts and 324 pages of secondary data form the basis for conducting our comparative case analysis. Although the methods used and the firms investigated varied across our studies, we consistently found the following: When responding to cross-channel shopping, multi-channel incumbents follow one of three distinctive strategic development paths. Successful players choose the path that best matches their strengths, current capabilities, and specific market conditions. Table 1.1 summarizes the characteristics of the sampled firms.

Table 1.1. Overview of Case Firms. Source: own graph.

Firm:	Number of Employees 2011	Revenues 2011	Distribution Channel Portfolio	Number of Interviews Conducted	Interviews Conducted by Management Type
Annapurna	< 1,000	< 200 mio.	Stores (22; 2011)* E-commerce (2006)** Catalog/call-center	14	Top management interviews: 3 Higher middle management interviews: 5 Lower middle management interviews: 6
Everest	> 10,000	> 2,000 mio.	Stores (434; 2011)* E-commerce (2011)**	9	Top management interviews: 4 Higher middle management interviews: 3 Lower middle management interviews: 2
Kilimanjaro	> 10,000	> 2,000 mio.	Stores (65; 2011)* E-commerce (2003)**	5	Top management interviews: 1 Higher middle management interviews: 2 Lower middle management interviews: 2
K2	< 1,000	> 200 mio.	Stores (50; 2011)* E-commerce (2011)**	7	Top management interviews: 2 Higher middle management interviews: 4 Lower middle management interviews: 1
Lhotse	> 10,000	> 2,000 mio.	Stores (1,200; 2011)* E-commerce (1999)** M-commerce (2012)**	4	Top management interviews: 2 Higher middle management interviews: 1 Lower middle management interviews: 1
Matterhorn	< 1,000	< 200 mio.	Stores (113; 2011)* E-commerce (1999)** M-commerce (2012)**	10	Top management interviews: 4 Higher middle management interviews: 4 Lower middle management interviews: 2
McKinley	> 1,000	> 200 mio.	Stores (21; 2011)* E-commerce (2007)** M-commerce (2012)**	4	Top management interviews: 2 Higher middle management interviews: 1 Lower middle management interviews: 1
Mont Blanc	> 1,000	> 200 mio.	Stores (16; 2011)* E-commerce (2002)** M-commerce (2011)** Catalog/call-center	14	Top management interviews: 2 Higher middle management interviews: 6 Lower middle management interviews: 6
Zugspitze	> 1,000	> 200 mio.	Stores (11; 2011)* E-commerce (2009)**	4	Top management interviews: 2 Higher middle management interviews: 1 Lower middle management interviews: 1

References

Accenture (2010). *Cross Channel Integration: The Next Step for High Performing Retailers*, white paper, Accenture.

Ansari, A., Mela, C. & Neslin, S. (2008). Customer Channel Migration, *Journal of Marketing Research*, 45(1): 60–76.

Bearing Point (2012). *C3 Retailing – Cross-Channel Commerce im Handel*, white paper, Bearing Point.

Berger, P.D., Lee, J. & Weinberg, B.D. (2006). Optimal Cooperative Advertising Integration Strategy for Organizations Adding a Direct Online Channel, *Journal of the Operational Research Society*, 57(8): 920–7.

Brunner, F. (2013). *Towards Cross-Channel Management: Strategic, Structural, and Managerial Challenges for Multi-Channel Retail Incumbents*, Dissertation No. 4210, University of St.Gallen, D-Druck Spescha: St. Gallen

Cavaye, A.L.M. (1996). Case Study Research: A Multi-Faceted Research Approach for IS, *Information Systems Journal*, 6(3): 227–242.

Chatterjee, P. (2010). Multiple-Channel and Cross-Channel Shopping Behavior: Role of Consumer Shopping Orientations, *Marketing Intelligence & Planning*, 28(1): 9–24.

Chiu, H.C., Hsieh, Y.C., Roan, J. & Tseng, K.J. & Hsieh, J.K. (2011). The Challenge for Multi-Channel Service: Cross-Channel Free-Riding Behavior, *Electronic Commerce Research and Applications*, 10(2): 268–277.

Deleersnyder, B., Geyskens, I., Gielens, K. & Dekimpe, M.G. (2002). How Cannibalistic is the Internet Channel?, *International Journal of Research in Marketing*, 19(4): 337–348.

Eisenhardt, K.M. (1989). Building Theories from Case Study Research. *Academy of Management Review*, 14(4): 532–550.

Eisenhardt, K.M. & Graebner, M.E. (2007). Theory Building from Cases: Opportunities and Challenges. *Academy of Management Journal*, 50(1): 25–32.

Emrich, O. & Rudolph, T. (2010). Cross-Channel Management 2011 in Deutschland und in der Schweiz, St. Gallen, *St.Galler Schriften zum Handelsmanagement*, St. Gallen:Universität St.Gallen.

Frambach, R.T., Roest, H.C.A. & Krishnan, T.V. (2007). The Impact of Consumer Internet Experience on Channel Preference and Usage: Intentions Across the Different Stages of the Buying Process, *Journal of Interactive Marketing*, 21(2): 26–41.

Frazier, G.L. (1999). Organizing and Managing Channels of Distribution, *Journal of the Academy of Marketing Science*, 27(2): 226–240.

Glaser, B. & Strauss, A. (1967). *The Discovery of Grounded Theory: Strategies of Qualitative Research*, London: Wiedenfeld and Nicholson.

Jick, T.D. (1979). Mixing Qualitative and Quantitative Methods: Triangulation in Action. *Administrative Science Quarterly*, 24(4): 602–611.

Konus, U., Verhoef P.C. & Neslin, S.A. (2008). Mulichannel Shopper Segments and their Covariates, *Journal of Retailing*, 84(4): 398–413.

Kushwaha, T.L. & Shankar, V. (2008a). *Single Channel vs. Multi-Channel Customers: Determinants and Value to Retailers*, working paper, Texas A&M University.

Kushwaha, T.L. & Shankar, V. (2008b). *Optimal Multi-Channel Allocation of Marketing Efforts by Customer-Channel Segment*, working paper, Texas A&M University.

Levy, M. & Weitz, B.A. (2009). *Retailing Management, 7th* Edition, New York: McGraw-Hill/Irwin Companies, Inc.

Martin, J.A. & Eisenhardt, K.M. (2010). Rewiring: Cross-Business-Unit Collaboration in Multi-Business Organizations, *Academy of Management Journal*, 53(2): 265–301.

Micros (2011). *From Multi-Channel Fragmentation to Cross-Channel Transparency: Creating Competitive Advantage in Demanding Retail Environments,* white paper, unpublished document.

Miles, M.B. & Huberman, A.M. (1994). *Qualitative Data Analysis: A Sourcebook of New Methods,* 2nd Edition, Beverly Hills, CA: Sage.

Neslin, S.A., Grewal. D., Leghorn, R., Shankar, V., Teerling, M.L., Thomas, J.S. & Verhoef, P.C. (2006). Challenges and Opportunities in Multi-Channel Customer Management, *Journal of Service Research,* 9(2): 95–112.

Neslin, S.A. & Shankar, V. (2009). Key Issues in Multi-Channel Customer Management: Current Knowledge and Future Directions, *Journal of Interactive Marketing,* 23(1): 70–81.

Pettigrew, A. (1990). Longitudinal Field Research on Change Theory and Practice, *Organization Science,* 1(3): 649–670.

PWC (2012). *Customers take Control: Multi-Channel - The Changing Swiss Retail Landscape,* white paper, PWC Switzerland.

PWC (2013). *Demystifying the Online Shopper: 10 Myths of Multi-Channel Retailing,* white paper, PWC Global.

Rangaswamy, A. & Van Bruggen, G.H. (2005). Opportunities and Challenges in Multi-Channel Marketing: an Introduction to the Special Issue, *Journal of Interactive Marketing,* 19(2): 5–11.

Roland Berger Strategy Consultants (2013). *Dem Kunden auf der Spur: Wie wir in einer Multi-Channel-Welt wirklich einkaufen – Chancen für Handel und Hersteller,* white paper, Roland Berger & ECE Projektmanagement.

Rudolph, T., Emrich, O., Böttger, T., Essig, E., Metzler, T., Pfrang, T., Reisinger, M. (2013). *Der Schweizer Online Handel – Internetnutzung Schweiz 2013,* IRM: St. Gallen.

Rudolph, T., Metzler, T., Emrich, O., Kleinlercher, K. (2014). Cross-Channel Management 2014 in Deutschland, Österreich und der Schweiz, IRM: St. Gallen.

Shop.org & J.C. Williams Group (2008). *Organizing for Cross-Channel Retailing,* white paper, Shop.org. and J.C. Williams Group.

Van Bruggen, G.H., Antia, K.D., Jap, S.D., Reinartz, W.J. & Pallas, F. (2010). Managing Marketing Channel Multiplicity, *Journal of Service Research,* 13(3): 331–340.

Verhoef, P.C., Neslin, S.A. & Vroomen, B. (2007). Multi-Channel Customer Management: Understanding the Research-Shopper Phenomenon, *International Journal of Research in Marketing,* 24(2): 129–148.

Yin, R.K. (2008). *Case Study Research: Design and Methods,* Thousand Oaks, CA: Sage.

Zhang, J., Farris, P.W., Irvin, J.W., Kushwaha, T., Steenburgh, T.J. & Weitz. B.A. (2010). Crafting Integrated Multi-Channel Strategies, *Journal of Interactive Marketing,* 24(2): 168–180.

2 The Strategic Perspective

"Don't force your customers to adapt to you.
Adapt yourself to your customers."
Anonymous

In the mid 1990s, the rise of the Internet was described as a disruptive development (Christensen et al., 1994). Predictions of the future suggest that consumers would buy most products and services though the Internet, bypassing classic bricks-and-mortar retailers (Porter, 2001). Recent developments prove that they were not entirely wrong. Online shopping has shown tremendous worldwide growth during recent years, and it is expected that online retailing will continue to outpace the growth of offline retailing. Up from $231 billion in 2013, U.S. online retail sales are estimated to grow by a compound annual growth rate (CAGR) of 10 percent to reach $370 billion in 2017. In addition, Europe's online sales of $166 billion in 2013 are projected to grow fractionally higher over the same period, hitting $247 billion in 2017, based on a compound annual growth rate (CAGR) of 10.5 percent (Forrester, 2013a; 2013b). However, the rising importance of the Internet for shopping offers tremendous opportunities not only for pure online players, but for offline players as well. New technological devices (e.g., smartphones, tablets) have enabled the advent of mobile-commerce and have further increased the influence of the Internet for offline transactions. Increasingly more shoppers display *cross-channel shopping* behavior, where online and offline channels are used interchangeably over the course of the shopping process – for example, to use online research for offline purchases. This offers considerable growth opportunities for multi-channel incumbents (Venkatesan et al., 2007; Konus et al., 2008). A number of consumer studies confirm that cross-channel shoppers are a more satisfied and, therefore, more loyal customer segment, and they spend, on average, three to four times as much as single-channel shoppers (Verhoef et al., 2007; Chatterjee, 2010).

In order to accommodate the demands of this lucrative segment, multi-channel players strive to interlink their online commerce with their store business, and thus initiate a strategic change process that includes various initiatives such as installment of cross-channel services (e.g., the offer "order an item online, and pick it up in a store of your choice") or alignment of the information systems and business processes (Accenture, 2010). Often, however, the anticipated success of this interlinkage has not been achieved, and firms are stuck in a change process that poses several management problems. This study identifies three key challenges. *First,* installed cross-channel services are costly, but fail to address customers' needs appropriately. *Second,* channel integration requires the alignment of current channel-specific managed systems and business processes that strongly challenge firms to reconfigure the architecture of their entire information systems. *Third,* because multi-channel firms are often organized in channel-specific business units with a profit-center logic, organizational design changes are needed in order to either increase collaboration among channel units, or to centralize and merge so far independent channel-specific departments (e.g., classic marketing vs. online marketing).

In response to these managerial problems, we aim to examine the strategic initiatives that multi-channel incumbents launch on their journey toward cross-channel management, and to specifically analyze how they are able to successfully manage this strategic change process. Thus, we ask: *How do multi-channel incumbents integrate their online and offline channels in order to successfully manage the firm-wide strategic change process in their move toward cross-channel management?* We developed a framework of four channel modes to answer this question, and to identify three strategic paths that multi-channel retailers can pursue on their journey toward cross-channel management.

2.1 The Four Strategic Modes of Channel Integration

On their journey toward cross-channel management, firms need to orchestrate their various consumer touch points. The strategic initiatives needed in the front end (e.g., diverse cross-channel services and cross-media promotions) and in the back end (e.g., alignment of information systems and business processes) are cost-intensive and can easily exceed the firms' available resources. Thus, if multi-channel players do not structure their identified initiatives and do not define a clear-cut development plan, they may encounter a painful transformation process, including budget problems, time pressure and over-challenged employees.

Based on our step-wise research design for examining how multi-channel incumbents successfully manage this strategic-change process, we were able to show that two dimensions are important for multi-channel incumbents when structuring their various strategic change initiatives, thereby setting priorities for planning their journey toward cross-channel management. The *first dimension* concerns the question of how to integrate all online and offline distribution channels with regard to strategic retail-mix characteristics (assortment, pricing, brand/layout, and promotions) in the front end. In the back end, the first dimension refers to the alignment of business processes and information systems such as order management/fulfillment, inventory management, and checkout systems (Zhang et al., 2010; Enders & Jelassi, 2000). The *second dimension* focuses on the integration of classic, digital, and social communication channels, and deals with specific tasks such as cross-media campaigns and means of marketing (e.g., promotions) in the front end and the alignment of channel-specific CRM solutions in the back end (Chen et al., 2005; Neslin et al., 2006). In fact, it is the interplay of both dimensions that determines an organization's state of channel

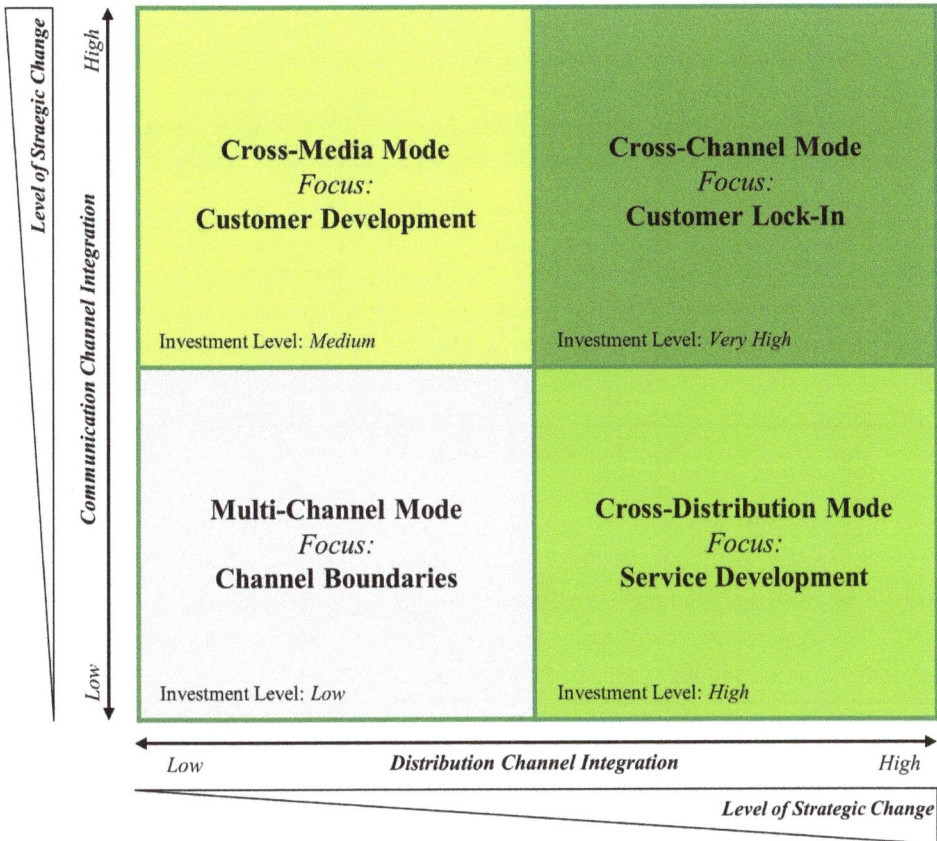

Fig. 2.1. Four Modes of Channel Integration.
Source: Brunner (2013).

integration. Within these two dimensions, there are four distinctive modes of channel integration (see Figure 2.1[4]).

2.1.1 The Multi-Channel Mode

Firms in the multi-channel mode still manage their distribution channels as separate profit-centers. Customers often find different assortments, pricing, and service levels across distribution channels. The same applies for channel-specific marketing and

---

4 The term "investment level" needs further explanation. Investment level means the investment costs for back end system alignments (e.g., CRM-system) or front end services integrating channels (e.g., in-store kiosk or in-store tablets for sales clerks).

communication means. In addition, channel units continue to run their own operational business processes and systems without sharing insights on customer preferences. Our research findings reveal that retailers in the multi-channel mode will forgo from ten to twenty percent of potential sales p.a. until 2015 if they are not ready to offer cross-channel services. Competitors offering cross-channel services or pure online players, in contrast, will increase their market share.

Everest – A German consumer electronics retailer exemplifies this multi-channel mode. For years, stores were the firm's sole distribution channel. Three years ago, after two unsuccessful trials, the firm successfully launched an online shop in addition to its store business. Because store managers hold a significant share of their own stores, they feared that cross-channel initiatives would boost the firm's online sales, thereby directly cannibalizing store sales. Everest recently introduced its first cross-channel service, where consumers can place an online order and then go to any store to pick up their order the same day. To the store managers' surprise, the result of this service was an increase in average customer spending in stores. Nevertheless, until now the channels have been managed as separate business units that have differences in assortment, prices, and layout in the front end, as well as having entirely separate processes and systems in the back end.

2.1.2 The Cross-Media Mode

Firms in the cross-media mode focus strongly on communication channel integration, whereas distribution channels are still managed separately. Bundling channel-specific consumer data into a centralized CRM system is a prerequisite for the development of cross-media campaigns and means of marketing that integrate classic, digital, and social communication channels. All cross-media activities are thereby aimed at simultaneously penetrating existing customers and acquiring new ones. A medium-level of investment is required, since firms mainly need to invest in a centralized CRM system. Typically, firms need from 12 to 24 months to establish such a consumer-centric approach across all communication channels.

Zugspitze – A German department store chain for premium clothing illustrates this cross-media mode well. The firm has traditionally relied on channel-specific CRM means, and has implemented a sophisticated loyalty card program. However, top management could not agree on the relevance of the cross-channel shopping phenomenon for their business model. Thus, they postponed the launch of cross-channel services and chose to integrate their online and offline communication channels in a first step. The firm has, therefore, invested in bundling its former channel-specific consumer data into a centralized CRM solution. Zugspitze is now able to compare store sales patterns with online sales patterns of more than 70 percent of all its customers in order to develop tailored campaigns or even personalized marketing promotions that better inform their customers. However, because Zugspitze is reluctant to integrate their distribution channels, the product assortment of the online shop is smaller than that of its stores, pricing differences continue to occur across channels, and channel-specific services are still predominant (e.g., the return policy does not allow customers to return online items in stores). Nevertheless, Zugspitze's success in the cross-media mode can be explained by their inspiring cross-media campaigns, as well as by the segment-specific personalized marketing promotions that are largely successful in boosting their store sales.

2.1.3 The Cross-Distribution Mode

Firms in the cross-distribution mode strongly integrate their distribution channels but only slightly coordinate their communication channels. They install innovative cross-channel services such as "Order an item online in the store and have it delivered home". However, such advancements in the front end require strong alignment of all relevant business processes and information systems in the back end (e.g., assortment planning, inventory management, replenishment). Our findings show that the necessary investment level in this mode can be considered high in comparison to the multi-channel mode. Furthermore, firms need between 24 and 36 months to align their business processes and information systems, as well as to implement cross-channel services.

Mont Blanc – The German sportswear and outdoorwear retailer is an effective example to illustrate this mode. Because the firm had to redesign its outdated channel-specific information systems (e.g., order management and fulfillment) and did not yet have a strong competence in using customer data, it was clear that Mont Blanc set the focus first on integrating their distribution channels. Although the cross-channel shopping phenomenon can still be considered to be in a formative stage, already 15 percent of overall Mont Blanc sales can be attribiuted to cross-channel purchases. This hardly comes as a surprise, however. Mont Blanc established in-store kiosks in every store in 2009, put tablets in selected stores in 2011. Also in 2011 the firm launched a mobile application that has already generated more than $1 million additional sales. Mont Blanc's success in the cross-distribution mode is at least in part a result of a very well-managed alignment of channel-specific business processes and information systems based on a firm-wide redesign project.

2.1.4 The Cross-Channel Mode

Firms in the cross-channel mode focus on both integration dimensions simultaneously. Our research indicates a very high investment level in this mode. However, in the cross-chanel mode customer loyalty can be increased more so than in the multi-channel mode, because consumers who switch channels while shopping build trust with the firms' cross-channel offerings. Thus, installing cross-channel services and developing personalized marketing promotions are key if cross-channel firms are to create customer lock-in.

Matterhorn – The Swiss retailer for entertainment products is a good example of this mode. The firm was facing a radical decrease in turnover of core product categories due to the advent of pure online-players such as Amazon. In order to remain competitive as a small and very flexible CEO-driven organization, Matterhorn decided to offer innovative cross-channel services while focusing on customer analytics for personalized marketing promotions. The focus on the simultaneous integration of both dimensions was driven by their aim to offer customers a convenient way to order online and use stores for convenient pick-up. Since 2010 when this strategic redirection was decided, Matterhorn has closely followed an integrated channel approach, treating all four distribution channels equally (stores, website, call center, and smartphone app), and customers used all four shopping channels interchangeably. Already, the cross-channel service "order an item online, and pick it up in a store of your choice" accounts for 17 percent of all online orders. Since its launch in 2011, this channel-switching service has generated twice as much traffic as the service "order an item online while in a store, and have it delivered to your home". Online activities have clearly increased store visits, and have fueled complementary sales. Moreover, the strongly aligned business processes and information systems not only enable Matterhorn to make product availability data accessible in real time across all channels, they also effectively address customers through personalized marketing activities. Thus, on the one hand Matterhorn's success depends on the installment of value-generating cross-channel services and the closely aligned information systems and business processes. On the other hand, their success also depends on effective personalized marketing promotions based on strong customer analytics competence and a powerful CRM system for collecting and analyzing a variety of relevant data.

Finally, we recommend that companies also evaluate the position of their strongest competitors in terms of cross-channel management. This action will strengthen their understanding of the market. If, for example, all competitors are ahead of the companys status quo and have already fully implemented cross-channel services, the threat of losing market share may increase significantly for the company. Furthermore, the results of the competitor analysis will help the company to choose a unique and appropriate path. If the cross-channel strategy is only a copy of competitors' plans, consumers will not see the added value. Such an analysis should help the company to improve its competitive advantage when pursuing the chosen cross-channel path.

2.2 Choosing the Right Path

Because most multi-channel players are still in the multi-channel mode while currently initiating a transformation process to integrate their online and offline channels, the crucial question is how to most effectively manage this top-driven strategic change process. Our research findings indicate that firms can choose from three different paths (see Figures 2.2, 2.3, 2.4).

2.2.1 Path I: "Attracting by Customer Inspiration"

This first path, "Attracting by Customer Inspiration," sets a clear priority for the integration of all online and offline communication channels over launching initiatives for distribution channel integration. The overall objective when following this path is to attract and inspire customers through cross-media communication and means of marketing in order to become a point of reference for a specific product offering, thereby increasing traffic in a preferred distribution channel as well as raising the potential for additional cross-selling.

> "Genuine cross-media management is based on the individual search and purchase history of customers and approaches each individual customer with personalized messages by using an optimal mix of classic, digital, and social communication channels." *(Zugspitze, a higher middle manager)*

Our empirical findings show that firms pursuing this path share the following characteristics. *First*, they are not directly challenged by pure online players attacking their market share, because customers prefer the store visit for their purchases (e.g., retail industries such as luxury clothing, high-end furniture, or cosmetics). Firms that are following this path prefer to stick to their channel-specific business model. *Second*, these firms usually rely on strong CRM competences with sophisticated loyalty programs and couponing initiatives in place. The customers of these firms are already accustomed to a high level of personalized marketing activities (e.g., personalized newsletters for specific events or promotions). *Third*, these firms try to leverage their strong marketing and communication competence to inspire customers to visit their stores.

Although many firms following this path are experienced in analyzing customer data and in developing channel-specific means of marketing, pursuing this path requires bundling of consumer data across channels and performing sophisticated analytics of various data sets to develop personalized marketing activities (Verhoef

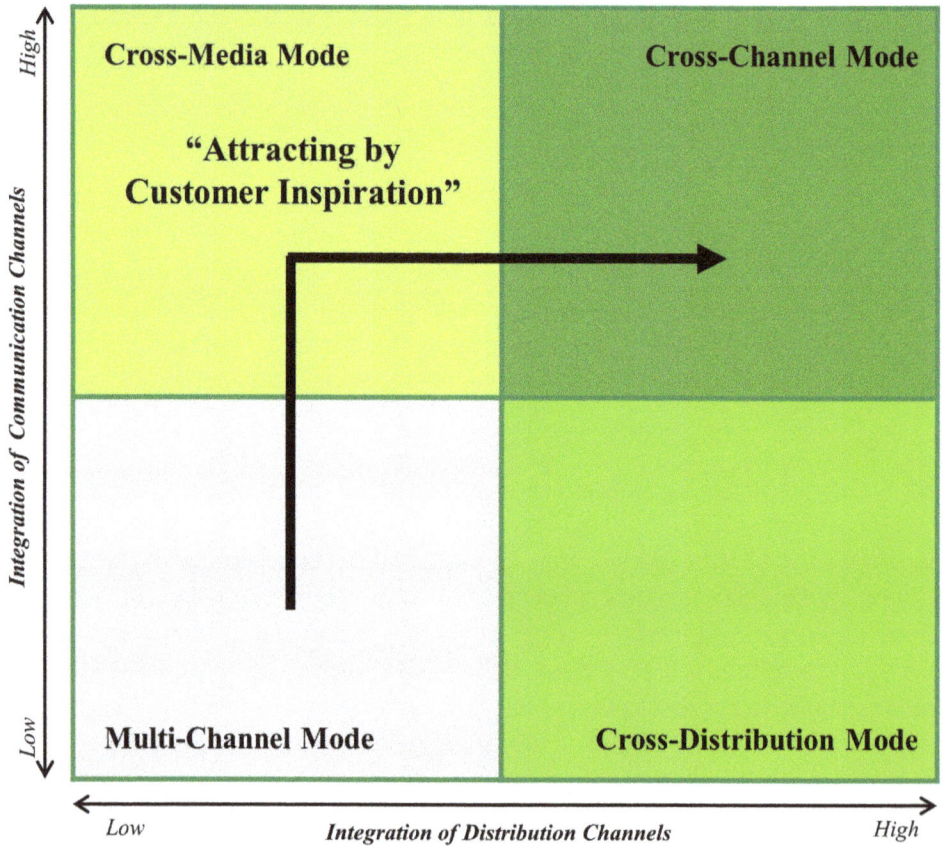

Fig. 2.2. Path I: "Attracting by Customer Inspiration".
Source: Brunner (2013).

et al., 2010). Thus, these firms need to gain knowledge on developing cross-channel marketing campaigns that involve various classic, digital, and social communication channels and that are tailored to segment-specific or even personalized consumer needs. In addition, because the firm-wide transformation process so far predominately concerned the marketing department, the organizational structure needs to be adapted slightly and reactively (Westerman et al., 2006). Firms prefer to stick to channel-specific practices while integrating and centralizing their separate online and offline marketing and merchandising teams. The focus on communication channel integration is, at first consideration, often thought to be less difficult than distribution channel integration, so firms tend to underestimate the complexity of performing the necessary consumer analytics and developing cross-channel means of marketing. As well, when firms become impatient and begin integration of communication channels prior to the integration of distribution channels, they increase customer expectations about cross-channel activities that are not yet ready to be de-

Table 2.1. Key Characteristics of Path I "Attracting by Customer Inspiration". Source: own graph.

Path I: "Attracting by Inspiration":		Representative Informant Quotes:
Key Capabilities:	• Consumer analytics	"Ideally, we have a strategy for each customer on what kind of promotions, at what time, by which means of communication to offer since we precisely analyze each customer's shopping patterns across all our channels." (Lhotse, a higher middle manager)
	• Cross-channel campaign management	"We use our mobile app as means of marketing to integrate various communication channels. In addition to the augmented reality function where users have the capability to scan a photo of their living room and then equip it with products in 3D from our online assortment, to make an online reservation for a personal shopping experience in a store of their choice, the link to send the configuration to a friend via email or Facebook is just one click away." (McKinley, a top manager)
Organizational Adapations:	• Slightly coordinated approach • Tendency to centralize and converge marketing and merchandising • Low level of cross-channel collaboration (purchasing, supply chain, sales)	"Until now, the offline marketing department manages all communication and promotion issues. It is also here where we will launch the cross-media campaigns in the near future. However, we are currently discussing whether the online marketing team shall be fully integrated into the offline marketing department, which will then be centralized." (Zugspitze, a top manager)
Barriers:	• Underestimation trap ⇒ customer confusion	"The design of cross-media campaigns that are strongly coordinated, content- and time-wise, is not as trivial as one might think at first. Particularly, the complexity of analyzing customer data to design target group specifics or even personalized cross-media campaigns or promotions is not to be underestimated. In addition, firms need to deal with the risk that customers already expect cross-channel services based on the cross-media activities, even though such channel-integrating services have not yet been installed." (Zugspitze, a higher middle manager)
Cultural Shift:	• Fairly low	"Although the degree of change is still low in the beginning of a transformation process, we have deliberately decided to involve all employees in the change communication." (Lhotse, a higher middle manager)

livered – which can lead to consumer confusion. Because the decision to prioritize the communication channel integration directly involves only the marketing and merchandising departments, the initial cultural shift within the firm is fairly small. Nevertheless, all examined firms following this path have set up a company-wide project to drive the transformation process toward cross-channel management (see Table 2.1).

2.2.2 Path II: "Delighting by Service Excellence"

This second path first focuses on integrating all distribution channels before tackling the communication channel integration. Firms following this path are driven by the notion that cross-channel shopping helps to defend the market position against pure online players if convincing and reliable cross-channel services are installed. Thus, the overall objective lies in striving for cross-channel service excellence.

> "At a certain point, we figured that we needed a clear plan on how to initiate the journey toward cross-channel management. So we decided to focus on the integration of channel-specific processes and systems to turn the whole firm toward service excellence, and then to launch a first cross-channel service with the installment of in-store kiosks." *(Mont Blanc, a top manager)*

The following characteristics describe why some multi-channel incumbents pursue this path when striving toward cross-channel management. *First,* they do not feel immediate pressure from pure online players, but instead perceive that consumers have begun to shop product categories online in addition to visiting stores (e.g., sportswear and outdoorwear, department-store line of products). *Second,* these firms usually do not use customer data to develop their means of marketing, and therefore lack advanced CRM competence. *Third,* they try to leverage their strong supply chain and business process competence by developing innovative and reliable services that enable customers to seamlessly switch between online and offline touch points during shopping.

To successfully advance along this transformation path, firms need to be able to adopt and implement new technologies such as in-store kiosks, tablets, or smartphone apps to launch cross-channel services such as "order item online in store, have it delivered home". In addition, the integration of distribution channels challenges firms internally, because fundamental business processes and information systems need to be completely redesigned – a project that is often time-consuming and costly, and affects daily business operations. Because the initiatives for integrating all distribution channels involve a firm-wide strategic change process, firms following this transformation path must adapt their organizational structure along the different channels (Westerman et al., 2006). The necessary intensified collaboration with purchasing and supply chains for all departments often requires complete reorganization. The distribution channel integration regularly reveals contradictions and ambiguities

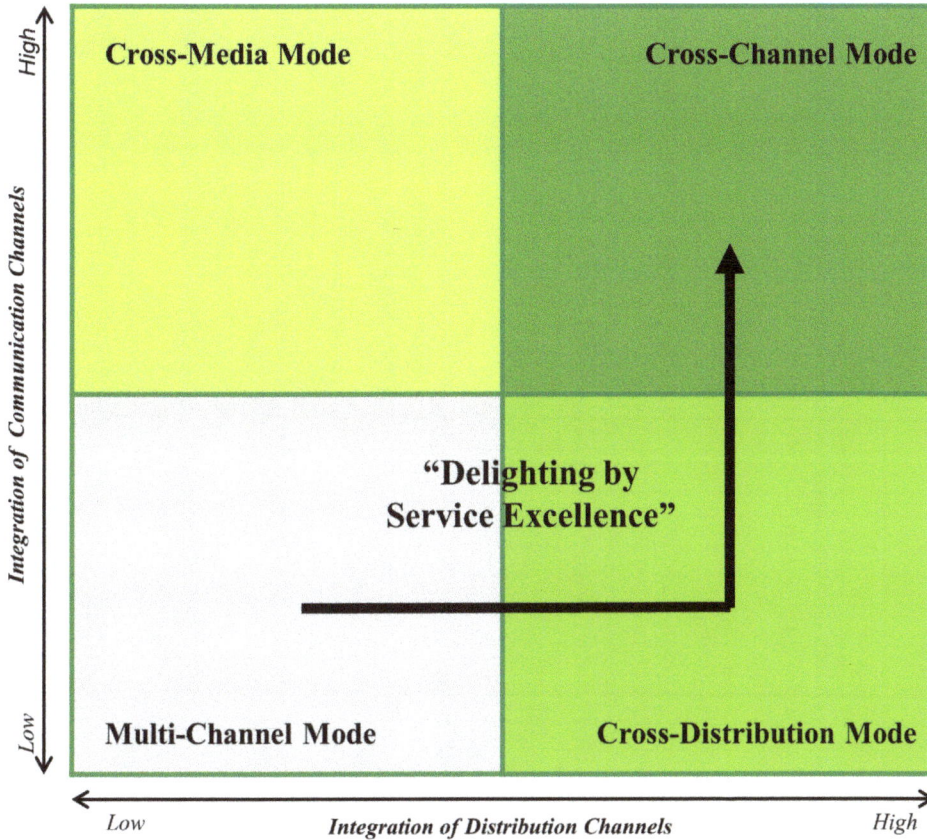

Fig. 2.3. Path II: "Delighting by Service Excellence".
Source: Brunner (2013).

related to channel integration initiatives, causing internal discord in the management team that lengthens the transformation journey. Instead of collaborating to find a fast and effective solution for business processes and system alignments, managers often become entangled in time-consuming arguments so that none of the redesign initiatives is effectively accomplished. These interlocking discussions increase the uncertainty level of employees and fuel fears that the online channel cannibalizes store sales (Deleersnyder et al., 2002). Although the management decision to prioritize distribution channel integration makes the transformational process explicit to all stakeholders in the firm, the cultural shift can still be qualified as rather moderate because the needed change initiatives normally last two to three years, leaving time for employees to familiarize themselves with the new business approach (see Table 2.2).

Table 2.2. Key Characteristics of Path II "Delighting by Service Excellence". Source: own graph.

Path II: "Delighting by Service Excellence":	Representative Informant Quotes:
Key Capabilities: • Technology adoption • Business process reengineering	"It is crucial to always try to be at the cutting edge of new technological innovations. And that's something we can be really proud of in our firm. In 2009, we were one of the first companies in Germany to have launched in-store kiosks in all stores. In addition, the early launch of tablets in their function as sales assistants for our sales clerks in 2011 illustrates that we have a high level of expertise in adopting and configuring new technologies into our business model." (Mont Blanc, a top manager) "The strong alignment of all business processes and information systems across channels will still strongly challenge the whole organization. This comprehensive screening of all back end processes and systems binds a huge amount of resources, and must happen in parallel to the daily operational routines that cannot be affected in any way." (Kilimanjaro, a higher middle manager)
Organizational Adaptations: • Strongly coordinated approach • Tendency to intertwine purchasing and supply chain • High level of cross-channel collaboration (purchasing, supply chain)	"It is absolutely necessary that all channel units and departments be more interlinked in the near future. In addition, the purchasing and supply departments of both online and offline channels need to be completely reorganized." (Annapurna, a top manager) "For the extensive interlinking of all distribution channels and the successful installment of cross-channel services, it is crucial that the management team fosters and even exemplifies the importance of cross-channel collaboration, in addition to the task of simply changing the incentive structure." (Mont Blanc, a top manager)
Barriers: • Absorption trap ⇒ channel cannibalization	"The management of the new SAP release and the launch of the tablets as a means to assist sales clerks are a real challenge. The launch had to be rescheduled several times due to management conflicts and unforeseen difficulties in the implementation phase. This, in turn, increased the general insecurity of our people and nurtured their fears about channel cannibalization." (Annapurna, a higher middle manager) Cultural Shift: ⊺ Moderate "It's not the case that we fundamentally change everything from one day to another. Although we are still at the very beginning of the integration process, we believe that this step alone will take approximately two years to be completed, since each and every process within the entire company needs to be analyzed and evaluated." (Kilimanjaro, a higher middle manager)

2.2.3 Path III: "Sprinting Forward by Moving Simultaneously"

Firms pursuing this third development path focus on the simultaneous integration of communication and distribution channels. The overall objective lies in speeding up the transformation process in order to benefit from a competitive advantage by offering a system of integrated online and offline channels.

> "The integration of distribution and communication channels was done in parallel. We adjusted all back end systems (especially the ERP and POS systems) to fully integrate all of our four distribution channels (stores, online shop, call center, mobile app) and also launched ten different cross-channel services based on a clear-cut implementation plan. At the same time, we started the bundling of channel-specific CRM data and developed a new logic for data analysis, as well as investing a lot of resources in the development of our first cross-media campaigns. You can imagine how the successful advancement of these simultaneous projects has challenged our company in addition to the smooth handling of everyday operations." *(Matterhorn, a top manager)*

Our empirical findings illustrate that firms following this path face very similar situations. *First,* they are heavily challenged by pure online players that are increasing their market share. Thus, firms are severely strained by radical decreases in turnover of core business segments, and are therefore forced to address both integration dimensions simultaneously. *Second,* customers begin to buy products online at significant levels (e.g., entertainment or consumer electronics products) and show interest in services such as online research and offline pick-up (e.g., online purchase and same-day store pick-up clearly shorten the regular delivery time compared to online orders). Customers are, furthermore, accustomed to placing online orders in addition to their store visits, and thus expect inspiring and customized marketing promotions from their store-based retailer of choice. *Third,* firms who set out on this transformation path have already achieved a high degree of maturity in aligning channel-specific information systems and business processes, and in integrating all customer data in one centralized CRM system. Firms following this path strongly believe that the cross-channel shopping phenomenon will boost sales, offering them an advantage over pure online players who cannot offer online-offline transaction services.

In order to successfully manage this demanding development path, firms not only need to possess the distinctive capabilities required for each of the other two paths, but they also need to focus on change management skills and external network competences. Because this path fundamentally accelerates and challenges every aspect of the predominant business approach and initiates a strong cultural shift within the firm, change management skills are of great importance. Firms therefore frequently collaborate with external partners. However, maintaining close relationships with each partner, as well as coordinating the various partners so that every outsourced solution fits the other elements in the channel system, proves to be difficult. In addition, firms are challenged to adapt their organizational design toward a lean, flat, and much more integrated structure. It is crucial that a small team consisting of top

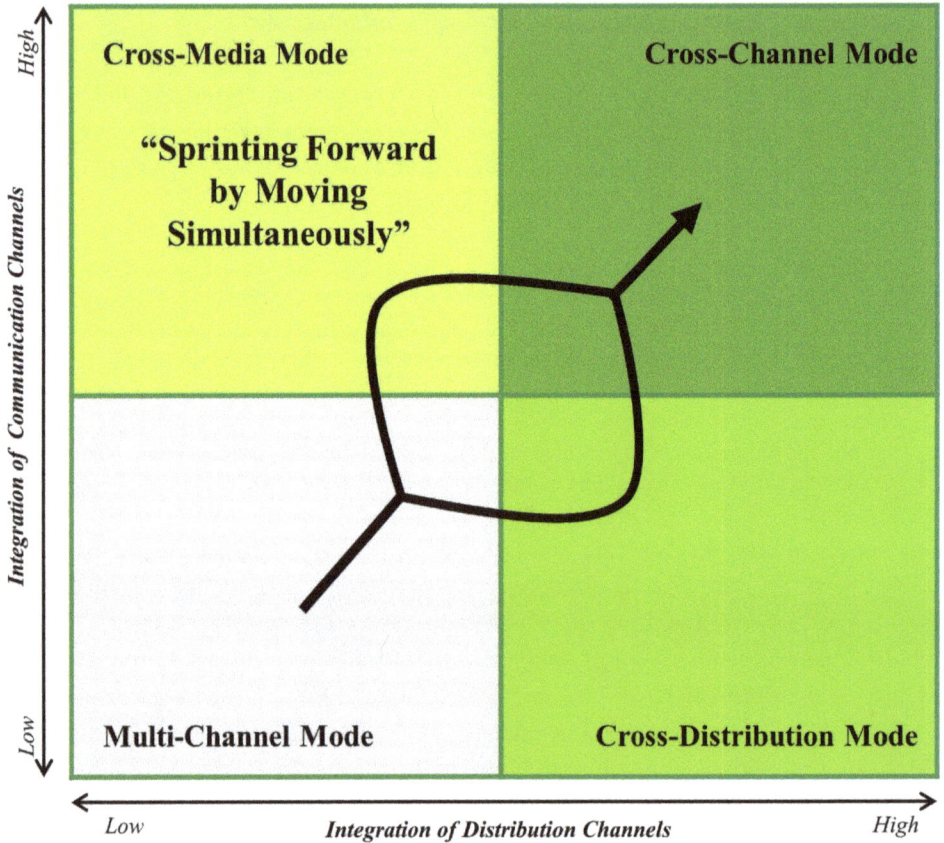

Fig. 2.4. Path III: "Sprinting Forward by Moving Simultaneously".
Source: Brunner (2013).

and higher middle managers be in charge of driving this change process. Moreover, because the various channels and their departments are more integrated and often centralized, the firm no longer needs to perform a high level of cross-channel collaboration. The focus lies on cross-departmental collaborations for specific topics (e.g., definition of the media spending plan). All examined firms pursuing this transformation path have established semistructural teams (Brown & Eisenhardt, 1997) that are responsible for driving the various channel integration initiatives. These temporary teams consist of employees who are assigned to fulfill cross-departmental tasks along specific guidelines, but with a high level of flexibility to act beyond regular everyday duties. Top managers need to make sure that they do not drive their organization beyond its current capabilities and swamp their employees, because relentless efforts to accelerate channel integration can lead to organizational exhaustion, individual indifference, and resistance. To prevent that, top managers must set up a rhythm of intense and less intense periods to grant employees enough time to adapt and regen-

Table 2.3. Key Characteristics of Path III: "Sprinting Forward by Moving Simultaneously". Source: own graph.

Path III: "Sprinting Forward by Moving Simultaneously":		Representative Informant Quotes:
Key Capabilities:	• Change Management	"With such a profound change of the firms' business approach, one must realize that the company is turned upside down. That's why you need good change management. In the top management team, we manage the transformation process based on the following guidelines: 1) provide a high level of commitment and a strong motivation to change, 2) communicate a clear vision and realistic goal-setting, and 3) create a sense of urgency with a strong call for an open communication culture." (Everest, a top manager)
	• External network competence	"The hiring of the external project manager and the very close collaboration with our external partners was crucial for the fast and efficient management of this transformation process. Internally, we would not have had the necessary knowledge to successfully manage this journey toward cross-channel management. Nevertheless, it is crucial to ensure that all developed solutions of the various project partners are, in the end, compatible with another, and that all project partners deliver comprehensive documentation on each project step to guarantee a smooth implementation." (K2, a top manager)
Organizational Adaptations:	• Integrated, semi-structural approach • Centralized and intertwined merchandising, marketing, purchasing and supply chain • Medium level of cross-department collaboration (centralized vs. decentralized units)	"As an organization, you must be lean and flat, and must work almost free of hierarchy. In addition, it is extremely important that you do not perish because of rigid structures. You need cross-departmental teams that can quickly adapt to changing conditions and intensify their collaboration for a certain time without any problems." (Matterhorn, a higher middle manager)
Barriers:	• Acceleration trap ⇒ employee resistance	"Based on a rough mind-map, we developed a structured plan. Then, we broke down the whole plan into distinctive project phases to prevent our employees from feeling swamped about the whole transformation process. These clear-cut project steps were easier to handle since we always allowed for a few weeks with no action between the intense project roll-outs." (Matterhorn, a higher middle manager)
Cultural Shift:	• Large	"Right from the beginning, we were aware that the whole project was very complex and that the change process would challenge the entire company. The launch of the online shop, the simultaneous installment of the cross-channel services, as well as the introduction of a cross-channel CRM system has, of course, strongly involved all departments. This change process has challenged not only the management team, but all employees as well." (K2, a top manager)

erate. Because this parallel integration effort can be seen as a fundamental change process for the whole organization, the cultural shift of the firm can be qualified as large (see Table 2.3).

2.3 Competing for the Long Haul

Our results indicate that the transformation process toward cross-channel management not only requires time, considerable financial investments and precise step-by-step planning, but also demands a high flexibility for change within the organization, driven through a strong commitment from top and middle management. This underlying in-depth case analysis brings to light several managerial conclusions.

First, the transformation process toward cross-channel management is not a quick-win move, but needs to be well-planned and structured. To illustrate this, we were able to derive two dimensions that a multi-channel incumbent can use to structure the already defined strategic initiatives. In addition, we were able to develop a framework of four distinct channel modes (see Figure 2.1) that help multi-channel retailers to both evaluate their status in the transformation process and to define which key challenges need to be addressed next.

Second, the developed framework helps to define the structure of the strategic change process toward cross-channel management. Based on that, we were able to identify three distinctive paths from multi-channel to cross-channel management (see Figures 2.2, 2.3, 2.4). To evaluate the success of the case firms in managing the transformation process, we identified the perceived change performance of top and middle managers, and related it to their chosen path, but we could not find a concise pattern to explain which strategic development path is more successful or more preferable than others. Thus, there does not appear to be an optimal development path to be pursued when striving for cross-channel management. Choosing the right development path seems to strongly correlate with the firms' existing strengths and current capabilities, as well as the specific market conditions. Nevertheless, our empirical findings still indicate the situations in which a particular development path may be more preferable than another. When firms are not ultimately threatened by the cross-channel shopping phenomenon, multi-channel incumbents can still stick to their channel-specific business model. In situations when multi-channel retailers are not dramatically challenged by pure online players (e.g., a segment for high-end furniture) but have a strong CRM and customer analytics competence, the development path "Attracting by Customer Inspiration" may be preferable. Furthermore, in situations where multi-channel players perceive that online-shopping is increasing in importance (e.g., regular apparel segment), retailers having a strength in the supply chain as well as in business process redesign may pursue the path of "Delighting by Service Excellence". Finally,

Evaluation Logic to Identify the Right Path:	Low	Medium	High
1. Online pure players dominate the market	1	2	3
2. Cross-channel services can generate a real value-add	1	2	3
3. We have a strength in customer relationship management	1	2	3
4. We want to develop skills in customer analytics and personalized marketing promotions	1	2	3
5. We have a strength in managing our supply chain across channels	1	2	3
6. We want to develop skills in redesigning our processes and systems	1	2	3

6–12 Points	13–15 Points	16–18 Points
Path I: "Attracting by Inspiration"	Path II: "Delighting by Service Excellence"	Path III: "Sprinting Forward by Moving Simultaneously"

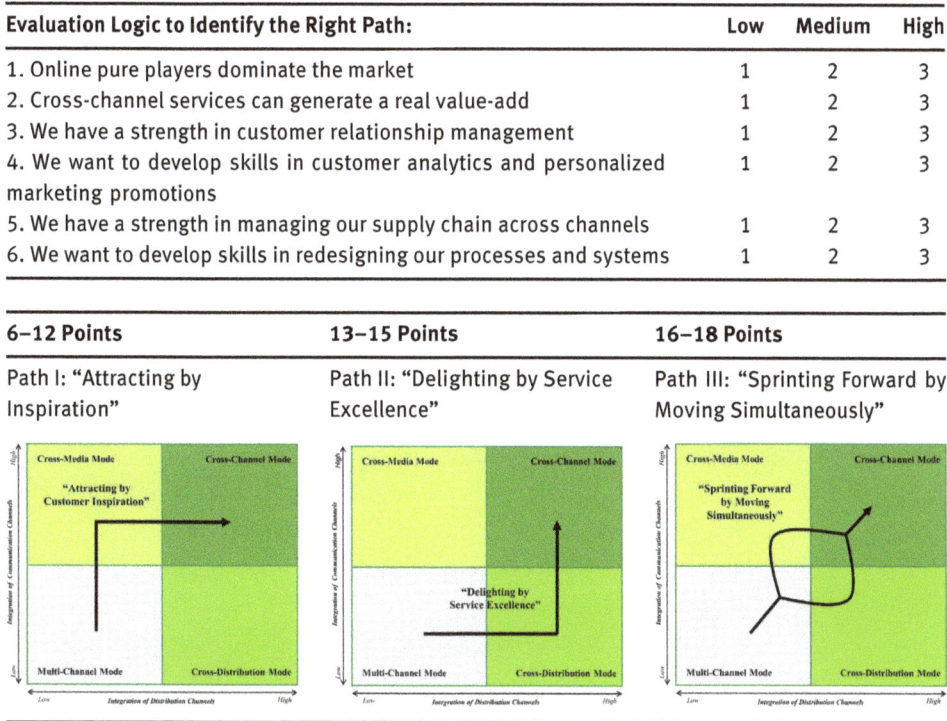

Legend: 1 = low; 2 = medium; 3 = high

Fig. 2.5. Evaluation Logic to Choose the Right Strategic Development Path.
Source: Brunner (2013).

in situations where pure online players evolve to become dominant market players, and where consumers are accustomed to shopping for their items online but may still see an added value in cross-channel services (e.g., segment of consumer electronics), multi-channel firms need to pursue the path of "Sprinting Forward by Moving Simultaneously". Based on our empirical findings, we developed the following logic that will help multi-channel incumbents to find out which strategic development path best fits their purpose to retain or even strengthen their market position in the era of cross-channel commerce. Managers should answer the six questions of Figure 2.5 in order to better understand the current situation of their company. The sum of the points will indicate a specific and optimal development path toward cross-channel management.

Third, our findings show that the cross-channel shopping phenomenon continues to offer tremendous potential for physical stores. Thus, excellent managed stores at great locations are crucial for multi-channel retailers when striving to intertwine their online and offline channels to install value-creating cross-channel services such as "order item online, pick up items in store" or "order item online in store via tablet or smartphone, have it delivered home or pick it up again in store".

Fourth, on the journey toward cross-channel management, multi-channel retailers face serious adaptations of their organizational structure, because the common practice of running online business as an entirely separate business unit is clearly outdated. In the short run, multi-channel incumbents need to at least coordinate their decentralized business units by structural means (e.g., installing cross-channel meeting structures) and decide whether the duplicity of channel-specific departments (e.g., online and offline marketing) should be resolved. Key departments should be integrated and centralized accordingly in the mid- to long-term planning.

The future of retailing will become even more complex. Besides identifying the best path toward cross-channel management and successfully pursuing the firm-wide strategic change process, multi-channel incumbents should not make the mistake of neglecting their single-channel target groups – customers that are still the source of the lion's share of their current profits.

References

Accenture (2010). *Cross Channel Integration: The Next Step for High Performing Retailers*, white paper, Accenture.

Brown, S.L. & Eisenhardt, K.M. (1997). The Art of Continuous Change: Linking Complexity Theory and Time-Paced Evolution in Relentlessly Shifting Organizations, *Administrative Science Quarterly*, 42(1): 1–34.

Brunner, F. (2013). *Towards Cross-Channel Management: Strategic, Structural, and Managerial Challenges for Multi-Channel Retail Incumbents*, Dissertation No. 4210, University of St.Gallen, D-Druck Spescha: St. Gallen

Chatterjee, P. (2010). Multiple-Channel and Cross-Channel Shopping Behavior: Role of Consumer Shopping Orientations, *Marketing Intelligence & Planning*, 28(1): 9–24.

Chen, Q., Griffith, D.A. & Shen, F. (2005). The Effects of Interactivity on Cross-Channel Communication Effectiveness, *Journal of Interactive Advertising*, 5(2): 19–28.

Christensen, C.M., Anthony, S.D. & Roth, E.A. (1994). *Seeing What's Next: Using Theories of Innovation to Predict Industry Change*. Cambridge: Harvard Business School Press.

Deleersnyder, B., Geyskens, I., Gielens, K. & Dekimpe, M.G. (2002). How Cannibalistic is the Internet Channel? A study of the Newspaper Industry in the United Kingdom and the Netherlands, *International Journal of Research in Marketing*, 19 (4): 337–348.

Enders, A. & Jelassi, T. (2000). The Converging Business Models of Internet and Bricks-and-Mortar Retailers, *European Management Journal*, 18(5): 542–550.

Forrester (2013a). *European Online Retail Forecast, 2012 to 2017*, white paper, Forrester Research.

Forrester (2013b). *US Online Retail Forecast, 2012 to 2017*, white paper, Forrester Research.

Konus, U., Verhoef P.C. & Neslin, S.A. (2008). Mulichannel Shopper Segments and their Covariates, *Journal of Retailing*, 84(4): 398–413.

Neslin, S.A., Grewal, D., Leghorn, R., Shankar, V., Teerling, M.L., Thomas, J.S. & Verhoef, P.C. (2006). Challenges and Opportunities in Multi-Channel Customer Management, *Journal of Service Research*, 9(2): 95–112.

Porter, M.E. (2001). Strategy and the Internet, *Harvard Business Review*, 79(3): 62-78.

Venkatesan, R., Kumar, V. & Ravishanker N. (2007). Multi-Channel Shopping: Causes and Consequences, *Journal of Marketing*, 71(1): 114–132.

Verhoef, P.C., Neslin, S.A. & Vroomen, B. (2007). Multi-Channel Customer Management: Understanding the Research-Shopper Phenomenon, *International Journal of Research in Marketing*, 24(1): 129–148.

Verhoef, P.C., Venkatesan, R., McAlister, L., Malthouse, E.C., Krafft, M. & Ganesan, S. (2010). CRM in Data-Rich Multi-Channel Retailing Environments: A Review and Future Research Directions, *Journal of Interactive Marketing*, 24(1): 121–137.

Westerman, G., McFarlan, F.W. & Iansiti, M. (2006). Organization Design and Effectiveness Over the Innovation Life Cycle, *Organization Science*, 17(2): 230–238.

Zhang, J., Farris, P.W., Irvin, J.W., Kushwaha, T., Steenburgh, T.J. & Weitz, B.A. (2010). Crafting Integrated Multi-Channel Strategies, *Journal of Interactive Marketing*, 24(2): 168–180.

3 The Planning Perspective

"The best way to predict the future is to create it."
Abraham Lincoln

Top managers of multi-channel retail incumbents are challenged to ready their firm for the age of cross-channel commerce. However, although a plethora of studies have been published on the change in consumer behavior toward cross-channel shopping, little is known about how to initiate and successfully manage this process. Confronted with this situation, top managers typically ask themselves the following questions: How do How can we manage this company-wide strategic change process? What should we specifically focus on along the transformation journey? How is the cross-channel strategy related to our corporate and business strategies? The research and empirical findings of this study lay the basis for two management frameworks that help tackle these very questions. These are 1) the *Cross-Channel Evaluator* and 2) the *Cross-Channel Flywheel*.

3.1 Management Framework One: "The Cross-Channel Evaluator"

With the *Cross-Channel Evaluator*, multi-channel retailers are able to assess how their industry is affected by the cross-channel shopping phenomenon, and how well their firm is already equipped to successfully manage the transformation process toward cross-channel retailing. The Cross-Channel Evaluator is a two-step assessment process that forces firms to evaluate their situation from both market and company perspectives.

The Market Perspective
In a first step, ten items derived from our own empirical data, extant theory, and studies (e.g., Gulati & Garino, 2000; Roland Berger Strategy Consultants, 2013) help firms to self-evaluate the relevance level of cross-channel retailing for their individual situation from an outside-in perspective. Based on a five-point Likert scale (1 - very low to 5 - very high), managers have to evaluate the competitive setting and consumer behavior in their industry.

To evaluate the change in consumer behavior, firms have to assess whether their customers are eager 1) to receive cross-channel promotions or 2) to be addressed by personalized promotions, 3) to research online and then purchase offline (classic ROPO), 4) to place online reservations for store pick-up, 5) to use online devices (e.g., smartphone, tablets) in stores, or 6) to return to a store items that were purchased online.

Table 3.1. The Cross-Channel Evaluator: Market Perspective.
Source: Brunner (2013).

MARKET PERSPECTIVE	Relevance level				
	Very Low	Low	Medium	High	Very High
Customer behavior					
1) Cross-channel promotions (e.g., digital coupon for store usage)	1	2	3	4	5
2) Personalized promotions (e.g., personalized newsletter)	1	2	3	4	5
3) Research online, purchase offline (classic ROPO)	1	2	3	4	5
4) Online reservation for store pick-up	1	2	3	4	5
5) Online-order in stores (e.g., smartphones, tablets)	1	2	3	4	5
6) Possibility to return online purchased items in a store of choice	1	2	3	4	5
Competitive setting					
7) Market share gains by pure online players	1	2	3	4	5
8) Other multi-channel incumbents striving for channel integration	1	2	3	4	5
9) Price awareness and margin pressure in the market	1	2	3	4	5
10) Customer inspiration as differentiator for multi-channel incumbents	1	2	3	4	5

Legend: ROPO = Research Online, Purchase Offline

Regarding the evaluation of the competitive setting within the respective industry, firms have to think about 7) the market share gains of pure online players, 8) other multi-channel incumbents striving for channel integration, 9) price awareness and margin pressure in the market, and 10) customer inspiration as a differentiator for multi-channel players (see Table 3.1). Furthermore, all named items are treated as equally relevant for the evaluation process.

Cross-Channel Relevance

0–15 Points	No immediate action required. You don't have to rush into the transformation process.
16–30 Points	Increased attention required. You should be aware that the integration of your offline and online business will become a serious management topic.
31–50 Points	Action required. You are in the position where cross-channel management is the strategic issue to be tackled immediately.

The Company Perspective

In a *second step*, twelve items derived from own empirical data and extant theory (e.g., Gulati & Garino, 2000; Booz 2012) allow firms to self-evaluate their specific level of cross-channel readiness for their individual situation from the inside-out perspective. Again, based on a five-point Likert scale (1 – very low to 5 – very high), top managers can self-assess their current channel strategy, organizational design, top and middle management leadership style as well as their company culture. To evaluate the present channel strategy settings, firms have to assess whether they must 1)

Table 3.2. The Cross-Channel Evaluator: Company Perspective.
Source: Brunner (2013).

COMPANY PERSPECTIVE	Readiness level				
	Very Low	Low	Medium	High	Very High
Channel Strategy					
1) Target group(s) for cross-channel growth are identified.	1	2	3	4	5
2) Assortment, pricing, and services are coordinated across distribution channels.	1	2	3	4	5
3) Promotions and campaigns are coordinated across all classic, digital, and social communication channels.	1	2	3	4	5
4) Key processes and systems are aligned (e.g., order management and fulfillment, inventory).	1	2	3	4	5
5) Customer data can be bundled and analyzed across channels (e.g., CRM and customer analytics).	1	2	3	4	5
Organization Design					
6) Current organizational design allows for strong collaboration across channels/departments.	1	2	3	4	5
7) Some corporate functions can be bundled and centralized (e.g., sales promotion, marketing).	1	2	3	4	5
8) Supply chain has a cross-channel focus (e.g., category management).	1	2	3	4	5
9) Incentive structure fuels cross-channel thinking on all levels and impairs cannibalization fears.	1	2	3	4	5
TMT-MM Leadership Style					
10) TMT leadership style fuels commitment to channel integration across all management levels.	1	2	3	4	5
11) MM on all levels are able to actively contribute to the transformation process.	1	2	3	4	5
Company Culture					
12) A culture of innovation, creativity, and learning motivates the workforce for cross-channel thinking.	1	2	3	4	5

Legend: CRM = Customer Relationship Management; TMT = Top-Management Team; MM = Middle Manager

have defined a clear target group(s) for cross-channel growth, 2) coordinate the assortment, pricing, and services across their online and offline distribution channels, 3) ensure that promotions and campaigns are developed on a cross-media basis by involving classic, digital, and social communication channels, 4) make sure that key processes and systems are aligned across channels on a company-wide basis (e.g., order management and fulfillment), and 5) are able to bundle and analyze customer data across channels. Regarding evaluation of the organizational design, firms have to 6) assess whether their current organizational design allows for strong collaboration across channels/departments (vs. silo-oriented business practices), 7) evaluate whether some corporate functions can be bundled and centralized (e.g., online and offline marketing), 8) identify whether the supply chain/category management has a clear cross-channel focus, and 9) ensure that the current incentive structure fuels cross-channel thinking across all management levels and impairs fears of channel cannibalization. Furthermore, concerning evaluation of the top and middle management leadership styles, firms have to evaluate whether 10) top management team's leadership style shows commitment for cross-channel management and 11) whether middle managers on all hierarchy levels feel empowered to actively contribute to the change process. From a cultural perspective 12), top managers have to judge whether or not the firm provides a culture of innovation, creativity, and learning that motivates the workforce across all channels (see Table 3.2). Also, in this case, all items are seen as equally relevant.

Cross-Channel Readiness

0–25 Points	Need for speed. You first need to tackle some basic requirements before striving toward cross-channel management.
26–40 Points	Keep on working. You are on a good path for setting the base for initiating the transformation process toward channel integration. However, do not underestimate the complexity of the change project.
41–60 Points	Good job. You are ready to think about launching inspiring cross-channel services that match your target group's needs. Watch out for differentiation against your key competitors and try to increase the share of wallet of your target group.

The Value of the Cross-Channel Evaluator

The two dimensions of the Cross-Channel Evaluator ensure that a firm is able to assess the relevance of the cross-channel shopping behavior in their industry context, as well as to evaluate their internal readiness to step into the area of cross-channel commerce. Therefore, the framework provides multi-channel incumbents with first insights into how to plan and structure the transformation process toward cross-channel management. The evaluation schemes of both perspectives should be used in companies. This allows managers to develop a common understanding of the status quo in terms of cross-channel management.

3.2 Management Framework Two: "The Cross-Channel Flywheel"

The *Cross-Channel Flywheel* is a process model that delineates how multi-channel incumbents should organize their firm-wide transformation process toward cross-channel retailing. It consists of nine distinctive planning stages. These are 1) change in consumer behavior, 2) review of business strategy, 3) market & competitive analysis, 4) strategic development paths, 5) front end configuration, 6) back end configuration, 7) structural adaptations, 8) middle management empowerment, and 9) cross-channel KPIs (see Figure 3.1). In the following, we describe each stage in more detail and point out the key questions managers have to address to successfully overcome

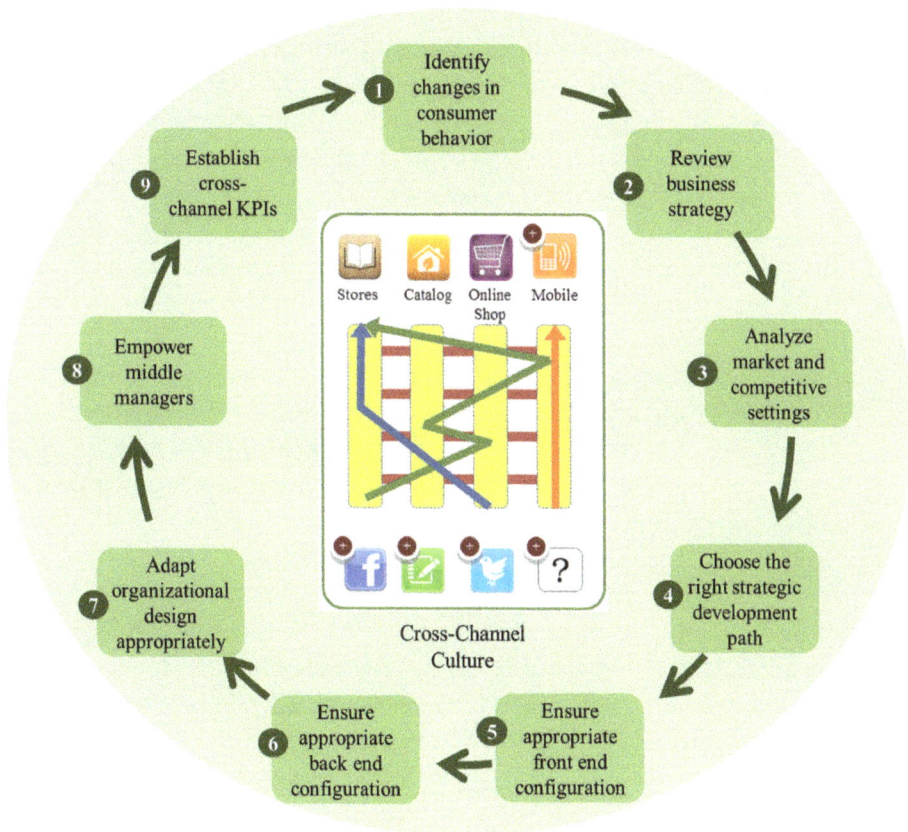

Fig. 3.1. The Cross-Channel Flywheel.
Source: Brunner (2013).

each specific process stage. We illustrate in each stage how the case firm Matterhorn has tackled the respective challenges.

Matterhorn is an entertainment products retailer from the German-speaking region of Switzerland. It is a very small and lean company that achieves sales per year of approximately $600 million Swiss Francs. It runs physical stores, a call center, and a well-known and highly accepted online shop. Since Matterhorn launched its fully equipped mobile commerce shopping channel in 2012, the channel system has managed four distribution channels – stores, an online shop, a catalog/call center, and a mobile shop. The firm recently launched an app for digital television as an additional distribution channel. The revenue shares in 2012 were as follows. Stores and catalog sales made up 70 percent of the revenue, with 20 percent of store sales being online-driven. The online shop generated 27.5 percent of the total revenue, with 10 percent of online sales being offline-driven. Finally, the mobile app contributed 2.5 percent of revenues – with a tendency to increase. Until the end of 2008, Matterhorn managed its distribution channels as clearly separate entities. When the online shop infrastructure faced severe performance issues following a dramatic increase in traffic due to online promotions, the former head of marketing was installed as CEO. He professionalized the online shop with a new release in 2009. Around the same time, the head of IT and processes convinced the new CEO to consider his idea of integrating the online sales platform with the store business, because he believed that a channel integration initiative would be the right answer for Matterhorn, to enable the company to defend its market shares against the upcoming competition from pure online players, and particularly from Amazon. Thus, after a revision of all key business processes in 2010, Matterhorn initiated their strategic change process toward cross-channel management in January 2011. By August 2012, almost all major change initiatives were successfully implemented.

Currently, Matterhorn can be considered a best-practice case for a multi-channel retailer that successfully guided its business into cross-channel commerce. Matterhorn consistently follows an integrated channel approach, with all four distribution channels treated equally and used interchangeably by shopping. For example, the cross-channel service "Order online, pick up in store" already accounts for 17 percent of overall online orders. Since its launch in 2011, this channel switching service has generated twice as much traffic as the service "Order online in the store, have it delivered to the home". Thus, online activities have clearly increased store visits and fueled complementary sales. The strongly aligned business processes and systems not only enable Matterhorn to effectively address customers through personalized communication means, but also to make product availability data accessible in real time across all channels. The firm has won several awards for its cross-channel approach.

3.2.1 Stage 1: Identify Changes in Consumer Behavior

In the first stage, multi-channel retailers need to assess how the change in consumer behavior toward cross-channel shopping affects target customers. So far, most multi-channel players striving for channel integration simply copy the cross-channel services (e.g., click-and-collect, order online in store, home delivery) from their core competitors instead of determining which services their customers would like to use. Our case studies showed, however, that successful players do not simply copy cross-channel services from their competitors. Instead, successful firms identify and anticipate the shopping needs and preferences of both existing and potential customers. Firms should therefore analyze the consumer decision journey (Edelman, 2010; 2013) of their defined target group(s). In addition, market research using qualitative or quantitative methods such as surveys, interviews, focus groups, observation, or even social media analysis (Facebook, Twitter) can help firms address customers more effectively by providing insight into what their own customers expect, and about how they can be meaningfully segmented in order to design better shopping channels. Thus, by analyzing the consumer decision journey of the most attractive target group(s), the multi-channel retailer is able to re-evaluate and sharpen the existing customer segmentation. Overall, the following questions must be addressed:

Key questions in Stage 1:
– What are the most attractive target groups for our firm? How can they be inspired by involving cross-channel services?
– How do existing and potential new customers from our most attractive target segment behave along their shopping decision journey? Which touch points do they use interchangeably along the buying process – when, why, and how?
– How can customers/customer segments be targeted in a customized approach?

Matterhorn identified as their most favorable segment female adults between the ages of 30 and 50 who buy entertainment products for the whole family, who are price sensitive, and who are beginning to use online and offline channels interchangeably. Analysis of the consumer decision journey revealed that the way this target group shops has fundamentally changed over the last ten years (see Figure 3.2). The following vignette illustrates the major changes in the decision journey of one of Matterhorn's target customers.

In 2003, Silvia is married, has two children, and is in charge of shopping activities for her family. One day Silvia's husband Karl heard the book *The Da Vinci Code* by Dan Brown being advertised on the radio. When he talked about this with his colleagues at work, he learned that the title was featured prominently on the bestseller lists and was even being discussed on television. After watching the television show himself, he asked Silvia to buy the book for him. The next day, Silvia spotted a coupon from Matterhorn in the local newspaper offering a special free bookmark with the purchase

Supplier of entertainment products (books, movies, music, and games)

Target group: female adults, 30-50 years, married, price sensitive, buys products for the whole family, uses online and offline channels interchangeably

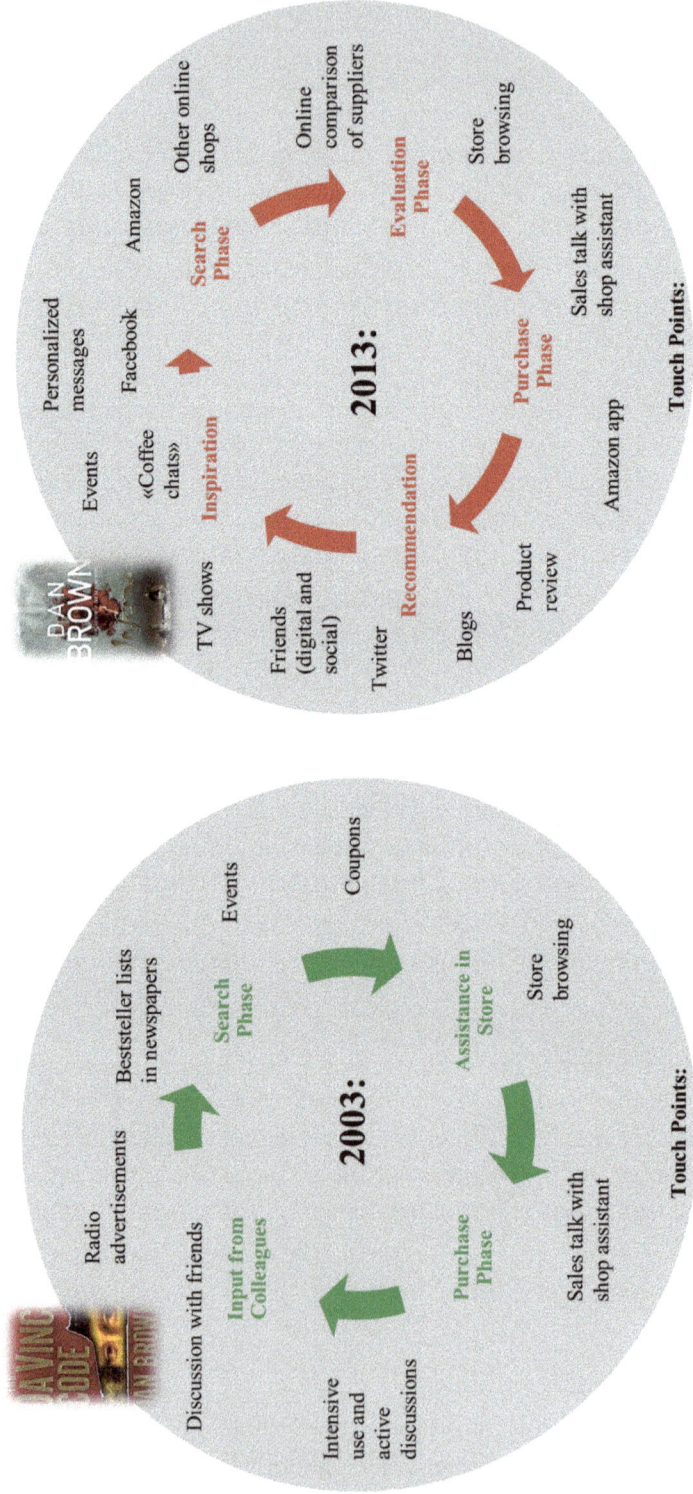

Fig. 3.2. The Consumer Decision Journey for Matterhorn.
Source: Brunner (2013).

of Brown's book. When she visited her favorite Matterhorn store to buy the book for Karl, she browsed through the book assortment and talked to a sales assistant. She used the coupon to buy *The Da Vinci Code* for her husband, as well as two other books she found when browsing through the store. Karl loved the book and was able to begin joining the conversation with friends and colleagues at work the next day.

Today, the situation looks entirely different. Karl is a big fan of the blockbuster movies *The Da Vinci Code* and *Illuminati*, both based on Dan Brown's bestselling novels. Karl is instantly excited when he hears about the new Brown novel *Inferno* through promotions on television, YouTube, and Facebook, and through a personalized newsletter from Matterhorn. The newsletter contains a promotional code that grants online access to a special audio feature with any purchase of a Dan Brown book. Karl texts his wife Silvia about the newsletter and asks her to buy the book for him as soon as possible. That same afternoon, Sylvia compares several book websites from pure online players and and from multi-channel retailers to find the best offer. Because the delivery time for the book on Amazon is more than three days, and all other offers are either more expensive or do not have suitable delivery times, she decides that Matterhorn's offer is the best one, as it comes with a free excerpt of an exclusive Dan Brown interview. She reserves a copy of the book online to pick it up a few minutes later in her nearby Matterhorn store. However, before picking up her order, she quickly checks the offer from Amazon once more via her mobile phone – just to make sure that Matterhorn really offers the best deal. Because she is still satisfied with Matterhorn's offer, she buys the copy of Brown's *Inferno* for her husband and – giving in to an impulse – also purchases another bestseller, *Die Totgesagten* from Camilla Läckberg. Karl is overjoyed to be one of the first of his friends to read the book. Over the weekend he posts comments about it on the literature blog he runs with friends, citing some passages from the book on Facebook and Twitter as well.

This example is a visualization of how significantly the consumer decision journey for buying entertainment products has fundamentally changed over the last ten years. Currently, various consumer touch points have to be synchronized and integrated to offer a seamless shopping experience across channels and the whole buying process.

3.2.2 Stage 2: Review Business Strategy

Before a multi-channel retailer initiates the cross-channel transformation process, it is crucial to review the business strategy to identify guidelines for the channel strategy. Rudolph (1993) introduces a framework for developing and reviewing the corporate strategy of a retail firm, and has derived three types of business model. These are 1) the global discounter, 2) the content retailer, and 3) the channel retailer. A retailer relying on a global discounter business model strives to be the cost leader through lean and efficient business processes as well as low prices (e.g., Aldi). In contrast, when applying the content retailer business model, retail firms focus on developing product innovations, aspiring to be product leaders in their market (e.g., Tesco or Zara). The channel retailer business model focuses on customer service, which is the reason why retailers who employ this model strive to become service leaders in their respective markets (e.g., Wal-Mart) (Rudolph, 2000).

Before defining the relevant change initiatives that lead to channel integration, the retailer's re-evaluation of the existing business model and value proposition should be based on the following questions:

Key questions in Stage 2:
– Do we still rely on the existing business model?
– Can we stick to the existing value proposition and, if not, how do we need to adapt?

When top managers of multi-channel retailers have reviewed their business strategy and have identified guidelines for developing their cross-channel strategy on the basis of the cross-channel value proposition, the actual planning of the strategic change process can be initiated. Although it is crucial to ensure top management's commitment for the cross-channel strategy to be developed, the case research shows that many multi-channel firms skipped this stage and began directly with the development of their cross-channel strategy. However, this can come at a high price when the established cross-channel services are not supported by top management or are not fully compatible with the business strategy of the firm, resulting in a weakened value proposition.

Matterhorn has always been selling books and music and has always instituted very lean organizational design and efficient business processes. Thus, the firm follows Rudolph's (2000) global discounter business model approach. Before initiating the strategic change process in 2011, Matterhorn's management team decided to retain this approach, but to adapt the value proposition slightly in the future. The aim was to actively promote a "convenience bestseller approach" based on developing a strong cross-channel competence as the key differentiator in the Swiss market for entertainment products.

3.2.3 Stage 3: Analyze Market and Competitive Settings

In the third stage, an in-depth analysis of the market situation will enable multi-channel retailers to define the right approach for coordinating online and offline channels. Because most multi-channel firms are confronted with an intensive market rivalry from pure online players or other multi-channel companies in their industry, they need to thoroughly analyze their competitive setting. Based on our collaboration with nine multi-channel retailers during their journey toward cross-channel management, we learned that the analysis of key competitors is often carried out quite effectively. However, most players neglect the knowledge they glean from analyzing the current market setting and future market developments that may be anticipated. To find answers to these crucial questions, it is important to identify the key drivers (e.g., digitalization, personalization, price erosion in the market) that may impact the definition of a cross-channel strategy, to explicitly evaluate how these drivers may change within the next three to five years and what the impact on the market setting might be. Having identified and evaluated the key drivers that define the market setting, multi-channel incumbents are able to decide how to differentiate their market position from competitors. However, because market and competitive analyses are often time-consuming, opening up a wealth of topics and issues which drive complexity and confusion, the following key questions shall serve as a guideline for multi-channel incumbents in Stage 3 of the cross-channel planning process:

Key questions in Stage 3:
- What are the relevant key drivers that help explain how our market will change in the future?
- What are the key initiatives of our main competitors (pure online players as well as other multi-channel players)? What can we learn from players of totally different industries?
- How can we differentiate ourselves from our competitors in order to defend or even strengthen our market position?

The key drivers influencing Matterhorn's cross-channel development are: 1) digitalization, 2) price erosion, 3) shrinking sales in certain product categories, and 4) new players. Figure 3.3 presents a visualization of these identified drivers to explain in more detail their expected development as well as their impact.

Matterhorn's key competitors who are also pursuing a multi-channel strategy are under great pressure. One competitor tried to sell its business in Switzerland but could not find a buyer, so as a result the company developed a costly expansion strategy. Two other competitors have recently merged. Pure online players such as Amazon and Apple have increased their market share.

Based on this market evaluation, Matterhorn tries to differentiate its market position through the following goals:
- Offering best-selling entertainment products with a good price-quality ratio
- Actively playing the "cross-channel card" by offering innovative cross-channel services
- Focusing strongly on convenience
    - customers can make an online reservation and pick up the product in the store of their choice on the same day
    - customers can make an online reservation or place an online order, but can pay the bill in the store.

No.	Driver	Short Description	Expected Development	Relevance
1	Digitalization	The market volume of digital media (e.g., audio books, music download, video on demand) grows significantly.	In the digital media market, Apple iTunes, Amazon, and Google are the players that dominate the global market.	***
2	Price Erosion	The average sales price for entertainment products has been heavily reduced during recent years.	The prices seem to recover slowly. However, the prices for Games will decrease even more. Some market players will face severe bottom-line problems due to this price erosion effect.	***
3	Shrinking of Product Markets	The market volume of classic entertainment products (e.g., book, CD, DVD) decreases heavily on an international level and strongly impacts the top line as well as bottom line of bricks-and-mortar and even bricks-and-clicks retailers.	As a consequence of this development, market players need to merge (e.g., Orell Füssli & Thalia in Switzerland) or even to exit the market.	**
4	New Players	Since online sales of entertainment products grew intensively during the last years, international pure online players (e.g., Amazon) entered the market and increased the competitive pressure for classic store-based retailers even more.	More pure online players operating on a global basis will enter the market and further facilitate the price erosion in the market.	**

Legend: *** = high relevance; ** = medium relevance; * = low relevance

Fig. 3.3. Relevant Market Drivers for Matterhorn.
Source: Brunner (2013).

3.2.4 Stage 4: Choose the Right Strategic Development Path

Because multi-channel incumbents will have to identify the cross-channel services they want to implement (Stage 5) and the systems and process alignments that need to be tackled (Stage 6), it is crucial that they determine how to set up the overall strategic change process. By using the derived framework of channel modes, as well as by relying on the identified strategic development paths (see Chapter 2), multi-channel incumbents are able to plan and specify the strategic change process. In addition, these strategic development paths allow evaluating various options on how to best structure the transformation process based on the defined strategic goals, the existing core competences, and other available resources. Thus, the framework of channel modes helps retailers to visualize planned strategic initiatives and facilitates the discussion of how to structure the strategic change process toward cross-channel management.

Since discussions on how to structure the transformation process towards cross-channel management can be complex and time-consuming, the following key questions may serve as a guide for multi-channel incumbents at this point:

Key questions in Stage 4:
– Which cross-channel initiatives have we already initiated or planned?
– Which channel mode are we currently in?
– Which strategic development path toward cross-channel management do we want to pursue?

The structuring of Matterhorn's cross-channel initiatives in the front end as well as in the back end shows that the firm focuses simultaneously on the integration of online and offline communication channels, as well as on distribution channels (see Figure 3.4).

Based on the fierce competition from pure online players and other multi-channel incumbents, the management team decided that the concurrent integration of both communication and distribution channels was the right development path toward cross-channel management. However, although the management team has to pursue the "Sprinting Forward by Moving Simultaneously" development path, it was viable to evaluate the decision by specifying: 1) the reason why, 2) the planned approach, 3) the key challenges, 4) the possible actions for overcoming these challenges, 5) the potential barriers to overcoming, and 6) the timeline for implementation (see Figure 3.5). This structure provides management teams of multi-channel players with an evaluation basis for deciding which strategic development path best fits their specific situation.

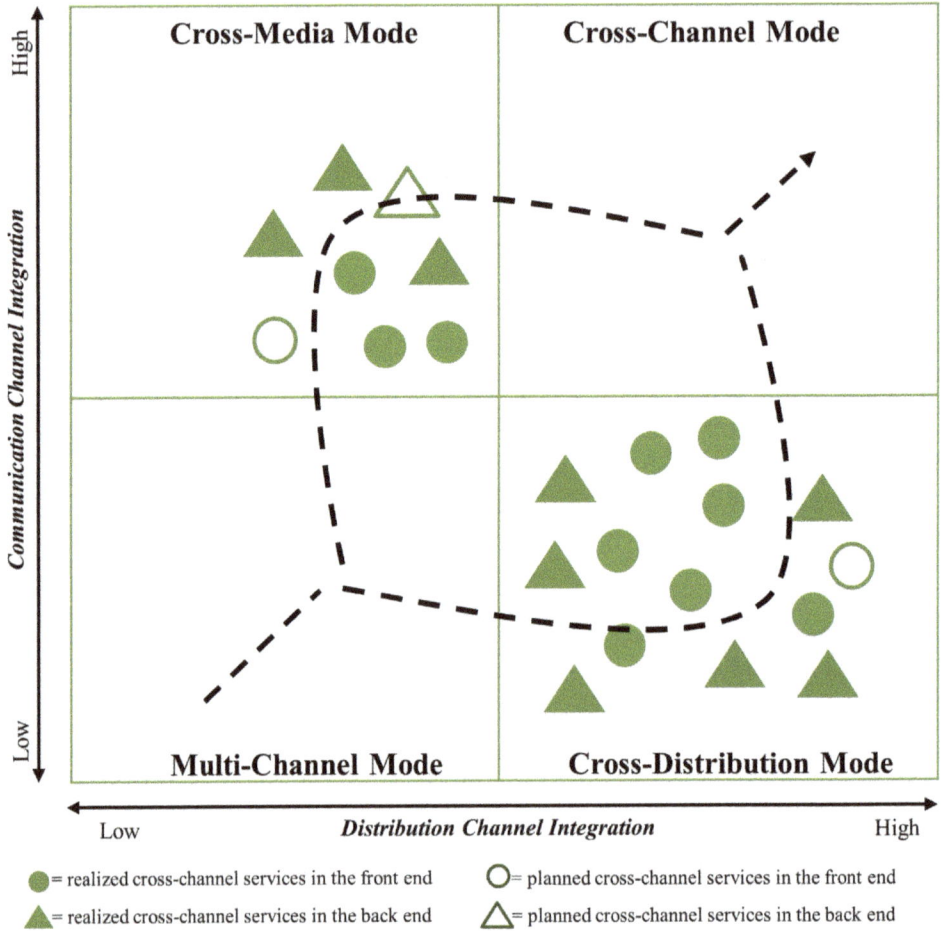

Fig. 3.4. Overview of Matterhorn's Cross-Channel Initiatives.
Source: Brunner (2013), based on internal documents from Matterhorn.

3.2.5 Stage 5: Ensure Appropriate Front End Configuration

In the fifth stage, multi-channel incumbents should define how they plan to coordinate, at the front end, both online and offline distribution, and communication channels. Based on findings from the previous stages, multi-channel retailers in this stage define cross-channel services that specifically attract and inspire their defined target groups, and that help to differentiate their firm's position against competitors. However, firms need to first discuss how the retail mix instruments should be managed across channels, and to do so they should tackle the following questions:

– *Assortment:* Do we offer the same assortment online and offline, or do we prefer a long-tail approach?

Strategic Development Path III: "Sprinting Forward by Moving Simultaneously"

1. Reason why:

- High pressure from the market (Amazon as category-killer, price erosion, digitalization)
- Lean and flexible organizational structure
- Very flat hierarchies
- Firm-wide evaluation of processes has accelerated the change process

2. Planned approach:

- Small project team (5 people incl. the CEO) to drive the change process
- Stepwise implementation of cross-channel services
- Strong involvement of lower middle managers (particularly store managers) before the launch of the cross-channel services

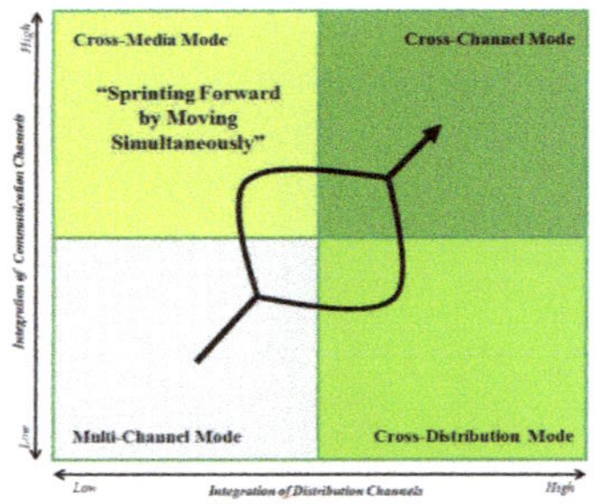

3. Key challenges:

- Cultural change actively addressed
- Management burnout because of workload
- Neglect of daily business

4. Actions to overcome these challenges:

- Intensive change communication by the CEO himself
- Intensive training of lower middle manager and employees
- Strong mutual support within the management team
- Jour-fix for "daily business only" on management level

5. Potential barriers to overcome:

- Channel-specific business approach
- Employee resistance

6. Timeline:

- Within 12 months, 21 initiatives, 14 implemented
- Within the next 12 months, rest of initiatives implemented

Fig. 3.5. Matterhorn's Reasons for Pursuing the Chosen Development Path.
Source: Brunner (2013).

Pre-Purchase Phase	Purchase Phase	Post-Purchase Phase
• Customers can use mobile devices to gather more information on product/services (e.g., usage of QR codes)	• Customers can place an online order to be picked up in a store location of their choice	• Customers are able to return items purchased online in a store location of their choice / at specified pick-up stations
• Customers receive advertising messages and promotions by way of various online and offline communication channels (e.g., flyer, email newsletter, Facebook)	• Customers can place an online order based on browsing the catalog (e.g., via QR code) or calling the call-center	• Customers are able to use the online return system for items purchased offline
• Customers receive personalized online messages with interesting store-offers or coupons to be used in a store location of their choice	• Customers can collect / cash-in loyalty points across all channels	• …
• Customers can check online for the availability of an item in a store location of their choice	• Customers can place an online order via a tablet pc/in-store kiosk	
• Customers can make an online reservation for an item in a store location of their choice	• Customers can cash-in digital coupons and promotions via smartphone when buying an item in a store location of their choice	
• Customers can browse the online-shop of the firm in a store location of their choice via tablets / in-store kiosks	• Customers receive a code on their sales slip to be cashed-in when placing an online order	
• Customers who are nearby a retailer's store location receive a personalized text message offering an interesting product	• Customers can place an online order to be picked up at a specific pick-up station (e.g., Swiss Post, Leshop Drive-In)	
• …	• Customers are able to pay online bills in stores and vice versa	
	• …	

Fig. 3.6. Overview of Innovative Cross-Channel Services.
Source: Brunner (2013).

- *Price:* Do we offer the same price online and offline, or do we try to maintain a price differentiation across channels?
- *Brand/Layout:* How do we ensure brand consistency – online layout vs. store layout?
- *Promotion:* How do we ensure that promotions are coordinated across all communication channels?

After answering these questions, multi-channel firms are ready to identify their cross-channel services. What has been learned from the case research is that successful players structure possible cross-channel services along the phases of the buying process in order to define which services they want to focus on. Figure 3.6 presents an overview of cross-channel services, based on the empirically collected case dataset and structured along the buying process that multi-channel incumbents can choose from.

However, the selection of innovative cross-channel services comes with two specific threats: *First,* the installed cross-channel services may not match the needs and wishes of the firm's target group(s), and therefore may fail to create customer value while creating sunk costs instead. *Second,* unmet desires and needs of target customers will be addressed by competitors' innovative cross-channel services instead. Figure 3.7 illustrates the two threats.

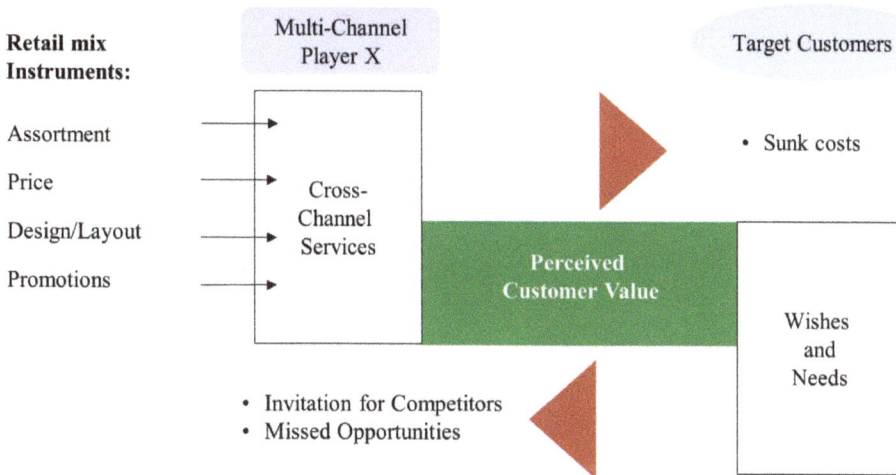

Fig. 3.7. Threats when Installing Cross-Channel Services.
Source: Brunner (2013).

To summarize, the following key questions must be addressed by multi-channel firms at this stage of the cross-channel planning process:

Key questions in Stage 5:
- How should we coordinate our online and offline distribution, as well as communication channels, according to the retail-mix elements?
- Which specific cross-channel services along the buying process have a high potential to inspire our target customers?
- How do we make sure that the selected cross-channel services offer strong potential for sustainable differentiation?

Matterhorn decided on a long-tail approach by offering more than 7 million products online versus 30,000 products in stores. In addition, the firm aligned their prices among all channels, decided to keep an eye on the layout so that the online-shop layout would display strong similarities with the store layout (e.g., color, design) and promotions could be coordinated across all communication channels.

Based on the definition of the retail-mix instruments, Matterhorn installed ten cross-channel services (see Figure 3.8). Six of these address the integration of online and offline distribution channels. In the pre-purchasing phase, Matterhorn's customers have the opportunity to 1) check in-store product availability online on a real-

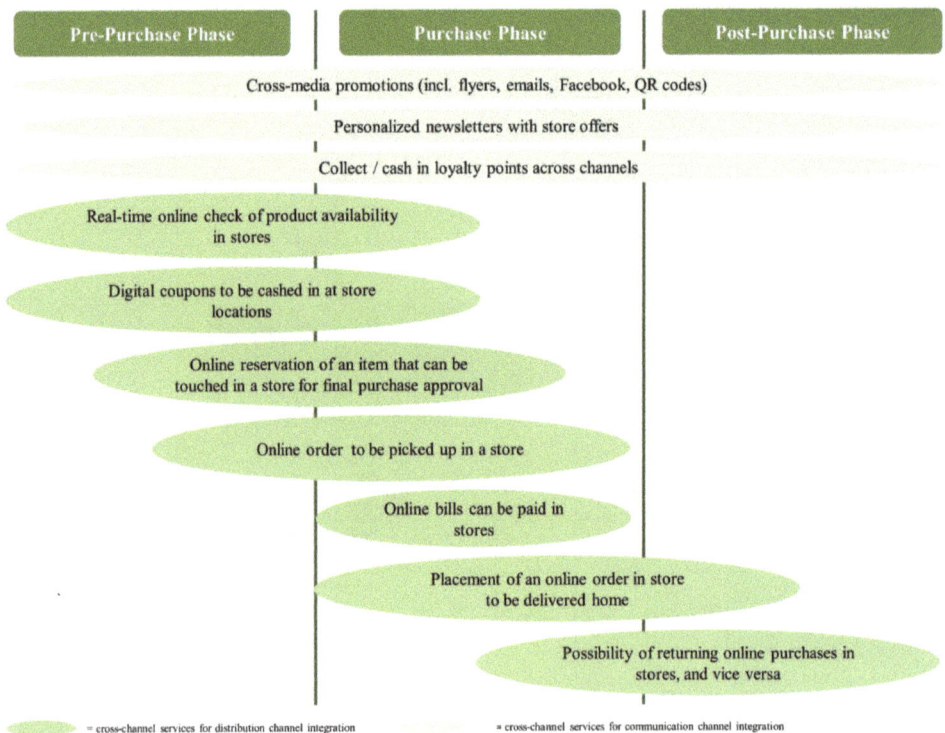

Fig. 3.8. Overview of Matterhorn's Installed Cross-Channel Services.
Source: Brunner (2013), based on internal documents from Matterhorn.

time basis and to 2) receive digital coupons by mail or text message to be cashed in at store locations. Between the pre-purchasing and the purchasing phase, customers can 3) place an online reservation for an item in a store and 4) even place an online order for store pick-up. In the purchasing phase, customers are able to 5) pay online bills in the stores. Between the purchasing phase and the post-purchasing phase, customers have the ability to 6) place an online order in store to be delivered home and to 7) return items purchased online in a store location of their choice and vice versa.

Moreover, three of these ten cross-channel services carry out a communication and promotion function along the entire buying process by integrating online and offline communication channels. 8) Cross-media campaigns and promotions, involving classic, digital, and social communication channels (e.g., flyers, loyalty cards, emails, text messages, Facebook, and QR codes) strive to inspire customer desires or to direct attention to new offerings by Matterhorn. In addition, customers are able to 9) receive personalized newsletters with attractive store offers and 10) collect and cash in loyalty points across channels.

3.2.6 Stage 6: Ensure Appropriate Back End Configuration

In the sixth stage, multi-channel incumbents need to decide how to align their online and offline channels in the back end (IBM, 2007; Martec, 2010). What we learned from our cases that were successful is the critical importance for multi-channel firms to transform their back end systems and processes from fragmented and isolated applications toward a service-oriented system architecture that structures their different systems and processes into three different categories. On the one hand, classic enterprise resource planning (ERP) systems such as inventory management, merchandise management, order management and fulfillment, customer relationship management, replenishment, and cashier management need to be strongly aligned. On the other hand, typical online-shop systems such as content management, product presentation and availability, shopping basket configuration, and banner management have to be strongly coordinated with the ERP systems. In a worst-case scenario, the online-shop specific systems do not communicate with the offline-based ERP systems, with the result that the online shop runs its own ERP system that is not compatible with the one from the store system. In addition, many so-called peripheral systems (e.g., supplier data systems, outsourced customer analytics programs, videos) also need to communicate with the ERP or online-shop specific systems. Thus, a multi-channel retailer's IT team typically has to ensure that approximately 40 to 60 systems and applications are structured and aligned so that the installed cross-channel services in the front end are based on reliable and scalable systems and processes in the back end. In their efforts to develop a lean, strongly aligned, and synchronized world of systems and processes in the back end, multi-channel incumbents should answer the following key questions:

Key questions in Stage 6:
– How should we align our online and offline channels in the back end?
– How can we ensure a lean and structured system architecture that is highly synchronized on a real-time basis and is stable for running the installed cross-channel services in the front end?

Based on the results of the process reengineering project in 2008, Matterhorn has begun to structure its back end systems and has created a system architecture along three pillars. The first pillar consists of all core ERP systems, the second pillar consists of all online-shop systems, and the third pillar includes all peripheral systems. Figure 3.9 provides a visualization of this approach, and serves as a reliable structure for evaluating the current system architecture of a multi-channel retailer.

Core ERP Systems	Online-Shop Systems	Peripheral Systems
• Merchandise management	• Product presentation	• Supplier data management
• Inventory management and control	• Product availability	• Content management
• Customer relationship management	• Shopping cart functionality	• Affiliate management
• Order management and fulfillment	• Banner management	• Customer analytics / newsletters
• Replenishment	• "My Account" functionality	• Locally based services / text messages
• Cashier management	• ...	• Social media (e.g. Facebook)
• ...		• Applications for barcode identification / QR codes
		• ...

Fig. 3.9. Three-Pillar Logic of Matterhorn's System Architecture.
Source: Based on internal documents from Matterhorn.

The first category, *Core ERP Systems*, aligns systems such as merchandise management, inventory management and control, customer relationship management, order management and fulfillment, replenishment, and cashier management. The second category, *Online-Shop Systems*, coordinates all systems that are related to the web performance, such as product presentation and availability, shopping cart functionality, banner management, and personalized customer accounts. The third category, *Peripheral Systems*, bundles and structures all other systems, such as supplier data management, content management, affiliate programs, customer analytics, locally based services, social media applications, and applications for barcode identification. Each system category bundles and aligns the illustrated systems on a modular basis, and is synchronized with the two other categories on a real-time basis. A comparison of two blueprints from the systems architecture of our case example (Matterhorn stores) and another multi-channel player (here named "company X") clearly illustrates how important the clear and lean structuring of the system categories is, as are the syn-

Matterhorn   vs.   Company Y

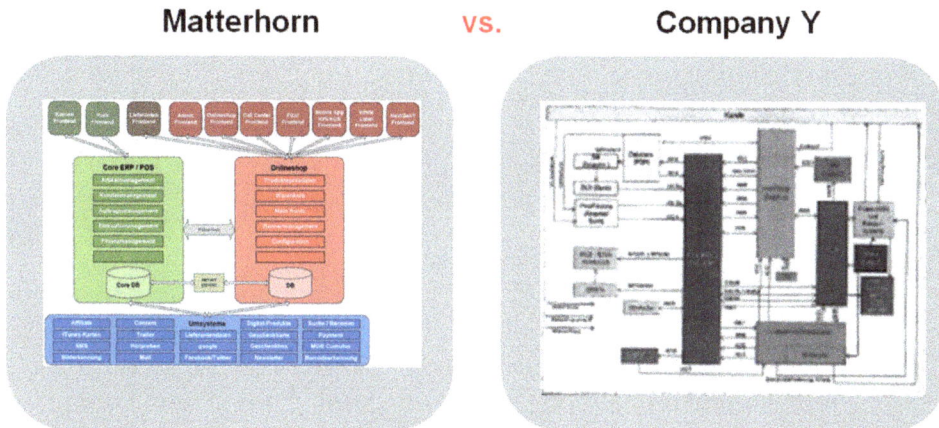

Fig. 3.10. Comparison of System Architectures.
Source: Brunner (2013), based on internal documents from Matterhorn.

chronization and real-time communication among the three systems category layers (see Figure 3.10).

3.2.7 Stage 7: Adapt Organizational Design Adequately

Since Chandlers' (1962) seminal study, it is well known that structure follows strategy. Thus, the chosen strategic development path *(Stage 3)* predetermines how the organization design has to be adapted. Using our derived framework, multi-channel retailers are able to evaluate which organizational adapation route they want to pursue, based on their chosen strategic development path. The following points summarize the questions that a multi-channel retailer needs to focus on when adapting organizational design toward cross-channel management:

Key questions in Stage 7:
– Based on the chosen strategic development path, what adaptations of the organizational design are needed?
– How do we ensure the successful implementation of these structural changes?
– How do we overcome change resistance among employees?

Because Matterhorn decided to simultaneously coordinate both, their online and offline distribution, as well as their communication channels, the needed changes in the organizational structure were fundamental and the firm pursued a *complete organizational design adapation* (see Figure 3.11). Over time, Matterhorn adapted its organizational structure from a channel-specific divisional approach to a department-specific functional design. Thus, the firm no longer operates with two channel units.

Route of Organizational Adaptation: "Complete Organizational Design Adaptation"	
1a. Adaptation of organization structure: • Change in organization structure from a channel-specific, divisional structure to a department-specific, functional design • Only sales units still follow a channel-specific perspective focused on the store business • Installed cross-departmental teams to drive change initiatives towards channel integration	**1b. Steps to reach the target structure:** • New function head of IT & Processes with its own department • Centralized category management in a new department purchasing / logistics • Online shop organization integrated in the purchasing department to leverage synergies between purchasing and product management for the online shop
2a. Level of cross-channel collaboration: • Low cross-channel collaboration • High cross-departmental collaboration; institutionalized by semi-structural teams with a lot of freedom to drive cross-channel initiatives	**2b. Actions to institutionalize it:** • CEO proclaimed that it is crucial that each management team member is involved in some cross-channel initiatives in addition to his or her daily business tasks
3a. Change in decision-making: • Moderate, since the management team is still making the important decisions • However, managers actively bring in their opinion in the semi-structured teams	**3b. Means to communicate:** • CEO as number one change communicator • Even store managers forced to bring in their opinions
4a. Change resistance: • Not very high because all management levels have advantages from the change in organization design	**4b. Actions to overcome change resistance:** • Regular and personal change communication by the CEO himself

Fig. 3.11. Matterhorn's Initiated Adaptations of their Organization Design.
Source: Brunner (2013).

It follows, instead, an integrated functional organization with centralized units of IT and processes, merchandising, and purchasing and logistics. Because Matterhorn has integrated and centralized their former channel-specific units, the firm no longer needs to perform a high level of cross-channel collaboration. However, a few cross-departmental collaborations remain in place since the strategic change process "took off" in 2011. By that time, Matterhorn had established small and flexible (semi-structural) teams for specific topics, consisting of passionate top and middle managers who were ready to meet the challenge of driving innovative topics on a collaborative basis alongside their daily business tasks, allowing significant freedom to self-structure cross-departmental topics.

3.2.8 Stage 8: Empower Middle Managers

At this stage, it is clear how the multi-channel firm wants to transform its firm toward cross-channel management *(Stages 3–7)*. However, because the retail industry is still a hierarchy-driven management setting, it is also clear that the strategic change process is likewise driven from the top. Top managers, therefore, need to win over the higher and lower middle managers, to motivate them to actively contribute to the transformation process. What we learned from our empirical analysis is that in the cases of successful firms, top managers not only involved their mid-level management in the strategic change process during the implementation phase, but they also empowered them to actively contribute in early phases of the transformation process by enacting three specific leadership activities. Our results explain how top managers of multi-channel incumbents are able to empower their mid-levels for active contributions along the whole transformation process – starting at the initiation phase, through formulation, to the implementation phase.

The following key questions allow a top management team of a multi-channel incumbent to evaluate the team's impact on mid-level empowerment in the context of the deliberate and strategic change in the process toward cross-channel management:

Key questions in Stage 8:
- Which leadership activities best support top managers' efforts to empower their middle managers so that they actively contribute to the strategic change process?
- Which actions actively prevent middle management disempowerment?
- How can top managers improve the informal top-middle management relationship in order to foster middle management empowerment and to drive assigned change initiatives?

At Matterhorn, top managers (including the CEO) were personally and intently engaged in the challenge of actively spanning hierarchy levels to convince mid-levels about the new vision to install the defined nine cross-channel services in the front

end. In this way the firm truly modelled the new cross-channel vision. Top management installed only a few guiding mechanisms, such as weekly steering committee
meetings where top and middle managers discussed the status of the change initiatives in great detail and decided – in a timely manner – on any necessary reframing
of goals or resources for the cross-channel services initiative. Moreover, to stimulate
feedback the CEO announced an open door policy for all top managers. Additionally,
he launched and joined implementation workshops with store managers to gather in-
put at the store level on newly developed cross-channel services and to get some ideas.
The following figure illustrates how the top management team of Matterhorn enacted
empirically derived leadership activities aimed at empowering their mid-levels for active contributions during the strategic change process. It further defines which actions
prevented middle management disempowerment, as well as those that stimulated the
informal top and middle management relationship (see Figure 3.12).

3.2.9 Stage 9: Establish Cross-Channel KPIs

At this stage, multi-channel firms need to define specific key performance indicators
(KPIs) to measure and evaluate the success of their implemented cross-channel initiatives. Currently, multi-channel retailers do not regularly measure the value of their
multi-channel initiatives (Aberdeen, 2010). This concern is made more challenging because both theory and practice lack insight into the KPIs that a cross-channel retailer
needs to focus on. However, based on previous findings (IBM, 2007; Arikan, 2008; Forrester, 2008; Unic, 2012), we developed a cross-channel dashboard consisting of four
structural dimensions that include 16 KPIs in total (see Figure 3.13). These dimensions
relate to Kaplan and Norton's (1992) well-known concept of the balanced scorecard,
and include 1) the customer perspective, 2) the financial perspective, 3) the marketing
perspective, and 4) the process and learning perspective.

The *customer perspective* consists of four KPIs. These are: 1) the number of CCCs
(cross-channel customers), 2) the spending level of CCCs, 3) the lifetime value of CCCs,
and 4) the loyalty level of CCCs. The *financial perspective* also contains four KPIs. These
are: 5) the ROPO I (turnover and number of orders for products that have been researched online on the website or on a mobile device, but purchased offline in the
store), 6) the ROPO II (turnover and number of orders for products that have been
researched offline via catalog or flyer, but purchased online on the website or on a
mobile device), 7) the TOPO (turnover and number of orders for products that have
been touched offline (in the store) but purchased online on the website or on a mobile device), and 8) the Margin Convergence (change in margin percentage points for
each channel based on the overall increase of cross-channel orders). The *marketing
perspective* also comprises four KPIs, which are: 9) the CCC acquisition rate (average
marketing spending to acquire a new CCC), 10) the POPO I (promotions online with
couponing or codes, purchases offline in stores), 11) POPO II (promotions offline with

Evaluation of Top Management Leadership Activities to Empower Middle Managers	
1. Activities fostering personal engagement: • Actively spanning hierarchy levels to communicate an live the new cross-channel vision • Building mutual relationship with middle managers and extensively supporting them in adopting the new cross-channel vision and communicating it to their subordinates **2. Activities providing structural guidance:** • Installment of a few but intensely used guiding mechanisms (e.g., steering committee meetings once a week) • Apply the principle of democratership, which means that each middle manager is heard, but in the end, decisions on adjustments of respective goals or investment levels are made by the CEO **3. Activities ensuring feedback accessibility:** • Launching and partaking in innovation workshops with store managers to get input on newly developed cross-channel services, as well as to get ideas	**4. Actions preventing middle management disempowerment:** • No blunt delegation of tasks to mid-levels • No policing of middle managers • No discouraging of mid-levels to provide feedback **5. Actions to improve the informal top management team – middle management relationship:** • The CEO connects directly and effectively with middle managers, and includes informal interaction • Use open-door policies and coffee break discussions as opportunities for top and middle managers to build relationships on an informal level • Create opportunities for many informal discussions between top and middle management

Fig. 3.12. Matterhorn's Approach to Empowering their Mid-Level Managers.
Source: Brunner (2013).

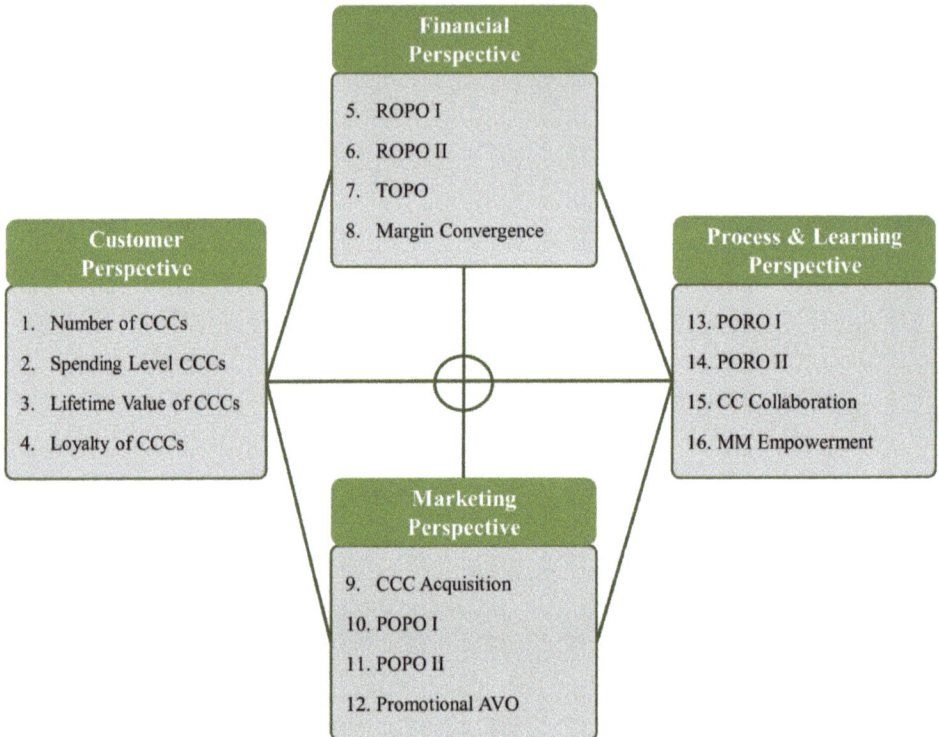

Fig. 3.13. The Cross-Channel Dashboard.
Source: Brunner (2013).

couponing or codes, purchases online on the website or on a mobile device), and 12) promotional AVO (average order value needed to generate revenue for a mail or email campaign, or for any customer promotion, so that it pays for itself). The *process perspective* again comprises four KPIs. These are: 13) the PORO I (service quality when items purchased online on the website or with a mobile device are returned offline in stores), 14) the PORO II (service quality when items purchased offline in stores or in the catalog are returned online via online support), 15) CCC (level of cross-channel collaboration among channels and/or departments), and 16) level of middle management empowerment (evaluated by middle managers themselves).

The cross-channel dashboard allows multi-channel incumbents to measure and evaluate the success of the implemented cross-channel initiatives in the front end as well as in the back end. For most multi-channel retailers, establishing a KPI dashboard to measure their success in cross-channel management is a major challenge. Often, the top managers of multi-channel incumbents are stuck in the multi-channel mindset and still evaluate their channel heads on the basis of channel-specific objectives – and thereby focus on multi-channel KPIS. The following key questions will help multi-channel retailers to establish a cross-channeldashboard:

Key questions in Stage 9:
- Which KPIs help to measure or to evaluate the various implemented cross-channel initiatives in our firm?
- Are these defined KPIs quantifiable, comparable, and value-driven, and do they revert to analytics data across channels?

At Matterhorn, the management team is currently establishing a dashboard with meaningful cross-channel KPIs. So far, the firm only measures the KPIs "ROPO I" and "TOPO". The cross-channel service "Online order, store pick-up" measured by "ROPO I" generated twice as many orders as the service "Online order placed in store, delivered home" measured by "TOPO". This means, therefore, that the online presence positively impacts the store frequency. That is already a crucial proof of concept pursuing a cross-channel journey. Nevertheless, Matterhorn has yet not been able to evaluate the spending level of their CCCs, or to quantify the overall lifetime value. Moreover, the marketing perspective as well as the learning perspective have not yet been adequately addressed. Matterhorn's management team is well aware of this fact and is currently implementing a dashboard with ten cross-channel KPIs specifically adapted to their business model requirements.

3.2.10 Cross-Channel Culture

Culture is a very important aspect along all stages of the cross-channel planning process, given that the transformation from multi-channel management toward cross-channel management initiates various changes within the firm. Culture is an emergent phenomenon that cannot be directly addressed or influenced (Schein, 1983). Therefore, the cross-channel culture rather is a result of the defined changes and actions in all stages of the firm-wide strategic change process than a variable that can be directly influenced.

Although *Matterhorn* is well aware of the fact that culture can not be directly influenced, it still tries to positively influence the cross-channel culture by encouraging informal and hierarchy-free discussions on fears and problems linked to the cross-channel strategy (e.g., during coffee or lunch breaks), by showing closeness and commitment to the cross-channel strategy among the top management team, as well as by installing multidisciplinary cross-departmental teams that are granted high latitude and a high-level of responsibility to successfully self-manage their assigned cross-channel initiative.

3.2.11 The Value of the Cross-Channel Flywheel

The Cross-Channel Flywheel allows multi-channel incumbents to develop their specific cross-channel strategy on a stepwise basis – taking into account the specific market conditions as well as the core competencies of the firm – and is thereby closely related to the business strategy of a firm. The framework incorporates an inherent logic. Thus, we strongly recommend that managers of multi-channel firms to address the presented stages of the process in the proposed order to successfully manage the transformation process toward cross-channel management.

References

Aberdeen (2010). *The Road-Map from Multi-Channel to Cross-Channel Retailing: The True ROI of Unified Customer Experience,* white paper, Aberdeen Group.

Arikan, A. (2008). *Multi-Channel Marketing: Metrics and Methods for On- and Offline Success.* Indianapolis: Wiley.

Booz Allen Hamilton (2012). *Winning the Multi-Channel Challenge: Customers, Channels, and Marketing Management,* white paper, Booz Allen Hamilton.

Brunner, F. (2013). *Towards Cross-Channel Management: Strategic, Structural, and Managerial Challenges for Multi-Channel Retail Incumbents*, Dissertation No. 4210, University of St.Gallen, D-Druck Spescha: St. Gallen

Chandler, A.D. (1962). *Strategy and Structure.* Cambridge, MA: MIT Press.

Edelman, D.C. (2010). Branding in the Digital Age: You're Spending Your Money in All the Wrong Places, *Harvard Business Review,* 88(12): 62–69.

Edelman, D.C. (2013). *Aligning with the Consumer Decision Journey,* available at http://hbr.org/web/ideas-in-practice/aligning-with-the-consumer-decision-journey, accessed May 30, 2013.

Forrester (2008). *Four Essential Metrics For Cross-Channel Measurement,* available at http://www.forrester.com/search?tmtxt=%20crosschannel%20metrics#/Four+Essential+Metrics+For+CrossChannel+Measurement/quickscan/-/E-RES46766, accessed May 30, 2013.

Gulati, R. & Garino, J. (2000). Get the Right Mix of Bricks & Clicks, *Harvard Business Review,* 78(3): 107–114.

IBM (2007). *Multi-Channel Retailing: The Route to Customer Focus,* white paper, IBM Global Business Services.

Kaplan, R.S. & Norton, D.P. (1992). The Balanced Scorecard – Measures that Drive Peformance, *Harvard Business Review,* 70(1): 71–79.

Martec (2010). *Multi-Channel Retailing 2010: Summary of Research Findings,* white paper, Martec International, BT Expedite, EPICOR.

Roland Berger Strategy Consultants (2013). *Dem Kunden auf der Spur: Wie wir in einer Multi-Channel-Welt wirklich einkaufen – Chancen für Handel und Hersteller,* white paper, Roland Berger & ECE Projektmanagement.

Rudolph, T. (1993). *Positionierungs- und Profilierungsstrategien im europäischen Einzelhandel,* St. Gallen: Verlag Thexis.

Rudolph T. (2000). *Erfolgreiche Geschäftsmodelle im europäischen Handel: Ausmass, Formen und Konsequenzen der Internationalisierung für das Handelsmanagement,* St. Gallen: Forschungsinstitut für Absatz und Handel.

Schein, E.H. (1983). The Role of the Founder in Creating Organizational Culture, *Organizational dynamics,* 12(1): 13–28.

Unic (2012). *First Results of the E-Commerce Benchmark,* white paper. Unic.

4 Outlook

During our research over the past four years, we learned that the journey toward cross-channel management entails a broad renewal of the entire firm. Against this transformative background, the future in retailing will belong to those firms that (1) manage to complete this transformation process in a timely manner and that (2) successfully and continually develop, manage, and improve a system of tightly linked online and offline channels. The following key insights from research and practice will offer an outlook on the challenges an opportunities that companies confront along the way.

The *first insight* is that digital devices are predominant in almost all daily activities. The example of current media interactions reveals that approximately 90 percent of daily media interactions are already screen-based – using either a smartphone, laptop/PC, tablet device, or television to locate information. The expectation for the future is that multi-device usage behavior will gain even more importance, and will thereby have a strong impact on cross-channel shopping behavior. In addition, we expect that consumers will be able to adapt to changes in technology much faster than in the past. Unfortunately, for firms this means that the life cycle of their offered products and services will become shorter also.

The *second insight* is that firms striving toward cross-channel management need to tackle the firm-wide change process actively and openly, and see the investment in cross-channel means as a long-term endeavor rather than a mid-length or short-term financial effort. Thus, the firms we examined that have successfully managed the transformation process display the following common aspects: Both top and middle managers were strongly convinced that cross-channel shopping is highly relevant for the company's future, and they were courageous and highly motivated to develop that future. As well, they were ready to tackle the inherent conflicts of the change process (e.g., store sales cannibalization, changes in organizational design, new distribution schemes to split bottom-line results). They wanted to be innovative and were ready to question every business process of the existing company. In addition, they anticipated that the investment in channel integration means might have a negative effect on sales and profits in the short-run, because cross-channel customers are more demanding and harder to satisfy. Firms pursuing the cross-channel path showed a higher potential for developing a competitive advantage, and thereby had increased chances to better penetrate their existing customers and attract new ones from their competitors.

The *third insight* is that cross-channel consumers desire to use only a few touch points, but touch points that offer compelling service functions for more than just one step in the purchasing process. Although many studies indicate that the number of touch points involved during the purchasing process will increase in the future, our empirical findings show that too many touch points offered by a retailer increases the risk of customer confusion. Thus, successful cross-channel firms thoroughly evaluate the consumer journey for their specific business, structure the purchasing process accordingly, and prioritize a limited number of highly relevant touch points.

The *fourth insight* is that the success of cross-channel players is explained by only a few, but highly attractive, cross-channel services that strongly support the firm's overall value proposition. Today, many firms feel significant pressure to establish a system of interlinked online and offline channels. Instead of focusing on their customer base and attempting to design differentiating services that support the firms' value propositions, they often just copy their key competitors' cross-channel services. The result is that such firms tend to install a bundle of rather generic cross-channel services (e.g., click and collect) within a short period of time, and are then surprised that the new services are not well accepted by their customer base. Our findings show that successful players focus strongly on their target customers' needs, identify specific services that match the firm's value proposition, and prioritize a limited number and often new services that do make an actual difference, adding true value from a customer point of view (e.g., specific digital services to interlink bricks-and-mortar with the online world).

The *fifth insight* is that unless structural and managerial aspects are adapted according to the new cross-channel strategy, cross-channel management will not be successful. By modifying organization design on the basis of a selected cross-channel path and a defined cross-channel strategy, firms can become successful cross-channel players. Successful top managers not only envision and communicate the new strategic direction across all hierarchy levels, but they also care about their middle managers when developing and implementing the defined cross-channel services. Moreover, they strongly encourage their middle managers to exemplify an "open door policy", and they proactively challenge their employees to be open to each idea or concern.

These insights shed light on the key aspects of an emerging phenomenon in retailing, which is still in its nascent stage. Yet many questions surrounding a successful and sustainable integration of online and offline channels remain unanswered at this point, and will be subject to further and extensive research over the next decade. However, what can be said with certainty, even today, is that in light of the current changes in consumer behavior, taking a static position is no longer a viable option. Top managers need to motivate their employees to proactively address these changes in consumer behavior. In addition, firms need to strive toward strengthening their value proposition with each newly launched consumer touch point or cross-channel service. A final but essential insight for the development of cross-channel management is that "Less is more". To successfully establish and manage a system of highly interlinked online and offline channels, firms must focus on few but highly relevant touch points, and develop specific value-adding cross-channel services that perfectly match the needs of their cross-channel target group.

About the Authors

Dr. Felix Brunner is a Senior Project Manager and a specialist for online and cross-channel retailing strategies at Migros in Switzerland. He earned his PhD at the Institute of Retail Management (IRM-HSG) of the University of St. Gallen, where he developed expertise in e-commerce and cross-channel retailing. His research interests include strategy process in disruptive environments, organizational design adaptation, and micro-foundations of dynamic capabilities in the retail context. Furthermore, he has an extensive background as a strategy consultant and trainer, coaching top and middle managers across various industries in strategy development as well as in the conception, implementation, and control of cross-channel strategies.

Prof. Dr. Thomas Rudolph is Professor of Marketing and International Retail Management at the University of St.Gallen. He is director of the Institute of Retail Management (IRM-HSG) and is the Gottlieb Duttweiler Chair of International Retail Management. He has written various books and over 200 articles in scientific and management-related journals, including the *Journal of Marketing* and the *Journal of Retailing*. In addition to his research and teaching activities, he has successfully established the Retail Lab, a partnership program between leading European retailers and the University of St.Gallen. Professor Rudolph has performed research projects for many noted international companies, including Ikea, Carrefour, Metro, Migros, Nestlé, Google, Aldi, and Swarovski.

www.ingramcontent.com/pod-product-compliance
Lightning Source LLC
Chambersburg PA
CBHW042108210326
41519CB00065B/7597